Scientific and Esoteric Encyclopedia of UFOs, Aliens and Extraterrestrial Gods

Volume III: A (Aliens-Ana Noura)
From a set of 20 volumes.
*** *** ***

Maximillien de Lafayette

Volume III
SCIENTIFIC AND ESOTERIC ENCYCLOPEDIA OF UFOS, ALIENS AND EXTRATERRESTRIAL GODS

The world's first and most authoritative encyclopedia of its kind!!

Published in the United States of America and Germany.

Printed by Times Square Press. New York.
Date of Publication: July 22, 2014.

Scientific and Esoteric Encyclopedia of UFOs, Aliens and Extraterrestrial Gods

Volume III: A (Aliens-Ana Noura) from a set of 20 volumes.

Maximillien de Lafayette

***   ***   ***

Times Square Press
New York   Berlin   Paris   Madrid
2014

Table Of Contents

Table of contents

Table of contents

*** *** ***

A

Continued from Volume II.

Aliens: Excerpts from vital information we received from the Grays (Greys), aliens and extraterrestrials in 1947.
Some are verbatim, and few are herewith produced with minor editing and revision based upon compared notes and translation by military scientists, two civilian linguists, and personnel who operated the aliens' communication devices.

Additional material and commentaries pertaining to the aliens' information and instructions are provided in various chapters of the encyclopedia.

Some data and information herewith listed appeared in other sections of the encyclopedia, nevertheless, the currect itemized list was found in a separate dossier from the AT (Aliens' Transcripts), for unknown reasons, consequently, reproducing the following information could be beneficial to the readers, in case they have missed previous listings.

The United States' governments has extensive files on aliens, as well as the aliens-humans equation from the dawn of the creation; the files, dossiers and vaults encompass every single thought, concept, theory and assumption on all aspects and facets of humanity, our origin, our history, how religions were created, how the concept of God was invented, the future of the human race, futuristic science, you name it.

The importance of ufology should not rotate exclusively around UFOs and exotic spacecrafts (Aliens or man-made); there are much more important subjects we should learn about, and focus our attention upon, such as our origin, the veracity of recorded history, and major (forgotten or missed) events in the history of humanity and planet Earth, our future/destiny, the influence and impact of galactic (aliens and extraterrestrials) civilizations on our culture, social systems, beliefs, our future and Earth's fate.

Fortunately, a great deal of information on these subjects were provided by aliens and extraterrestrials we have met on numerous occasions.

Herewith are some mind-blowing excerpts from the transcripts.

On the universe and multiple dimensions:

The universe was created from within; an implosion on the inside and collisions of bubbles on the outside. The universe emerged from a state of "Nothingness", told us an alien.

There are multiple dimensions beyond our physical world. And within each layer of dimension, there is a multitude of other forms of dimensions.

1-There are multiple dimensions in the universe, such as:

a-Parallel dimension,

b-Ultra dimension,

c-Adjacent zone,

d-Etheric zone,

e-Future's dimension,

f-Plasmic zone,

g-Time dimension,

h-And there are 12 interconnected dimensions that are constantly expanding. These zones and dimensions vary from one galaxy to another.

2-Black holes as well as white holes contain dark energy, white energy, dark matter, and neutral matter, gravity and anti-gravity, and time-space memory.

3-The universe-space has its own memory. It transcends space and time.

4-There are 224 planets that sustain life as we know it. (Note: Of course, this number has changed since 1947.)

5-The universe bends on itself.

6-Dark matter is what keeps the universe in place and in order, and contributes to its expansion.

7-The shortest distance between A and B is not a straight line, but a bent trajectory between two dots on a parallel plane.

8-Each galaxy contains millions of time-space trajectories.

9-In some dimensions, future does not exist, and in some other dimensions, the past is not created yet.

10-Our universe is one of many in the 'multiverse'. And the multiuniverse bends on itself and bumps into its multi-layers, thus constantly creating more universes, including galaxies, and black holes.

This item was mentioned twice in the Aliens Transcript and had 2 separate footnotes.

11-Einstein's general theory of relativity is not totally correct. It is only applicable to space-zones regulated by light and motion in one direction.

12-The universe expands in multiple directions, through the "dark energy flow". And if the universe ceases to exist, copies of the extinct universe will re-animate a new beginning that will explode into billions of new universes.

13-At one point in the universe, some galaxies were flat. And in the dark space of these galaxies, other time-spaces universes are constantly created.

14-Parallel universes although they are not visible to us have major effect on our psyche and eventually the future and fate of the human race.

15-Other universes leak their gravity into our world through the dilatation of "Time-Orbits" (Ba'abs). This gravity has time-space memory.

16-The big bang theory is incorrect.

17-The universe was created from an implosion originally rooted into the vacuum of nothingness, without time, space, past, and beginning. It exploded in the state of nothingness, thus it has no beginning and no end.

Implosion and collision of bubbles created billions of stars and planets. This item was mentioned before and noted twice in the Aliens Transcripts, with a minor variation.

18-We can enter a meta space-time zone, and observe what it is going to happen to planet Earth, millions of years in the future, because that zone is the original picture-dimension-existence of Earth. That zone in the future is the primordial existence of planet Earth. It is the same all over the universe. Each zone is a duplicate of another; this is how the Grays explained the infinity and ever-lasting expansion of the universe.

19-There are copies of each one of us in other dimensions.

20-On other planets, in our galaxy and beyond, and particularly in multi-dimensional zones or time-space zones, past, present and future concurrently exist on the same plane. This multi-co-existences allow other species to navigate time, back and forth in no-time.

21-Planet Earth will cease to exist in 5 billion years, along with our solar system.

22-There are several Ba'abs (Stargates) around planet Earth. These are the gates to parallel universes. New York and Chicago have several Ba'abs.

On the Moon:

1-There are "artificial" settlements and tunnels inside the Moon.

2-Many regions inside the Moon are filled with life-forms.

3-The Grays told the military how to get to the Moon in minutes, using "Route Orbital X", as called in the Aliens Transcripts. This route is accessible once every 25 years from Earth, and 7 years from Mars, unless they use the Ba'ab.

There are several Ba'abs around planet Earth. These are the gates to parallel universes. Although there is no wind on the Moon, it could be created from dark energy and channeled to the Moon.

4-At one time, the Anunnaki had settlements on the Moon and Mars. The Anunnaki built stations on the Moon and Mars before they landed on Earth.

5-The Moon will cease to exist in 5 billion years, along with Earth.

On our planet, Earth's monuments and primordial civilizations:

1-Earth axe shifted 4 times before.

2-At the very beginning, Earth had the shape of an egg. It was never totally round.

3-The Grays saved planet Earth from annihilation when they redirect the trajectory of a huge celestial body heading toward Earth. This happened twice in Earth's history.

Meteors or other celestial bodies did not kill the dinosaurs. It never happened.

4-The Pyramids are 10,900-11,000 year old. And were not built by the Egyptians or any human race. The stones were teleported.

5-The Anunnaki created the Euphrates and Tiger Rivers. And for a long time could not control their flow. This led to periodic floods; one of them is the great regional deluge in the Middle East.

6-Civilization was not created by the Mesopotamians. It was exported to their lands by the Anatolians (Plateau of Turkey), and the early inhabitants of Phoenicia, at a time this land had no name. Later on it was called Leebaan, Lubanana which means snow-white.

Civilization did not start in Mesopotamia, but first in Anatolia (Part Turkey, part ancient Armenia), continued in Phoenicia, and later on bloomed in Mesopotamia. Turkey and the Anatolian Plateau gave birth to the first form of civilization on Earth.

7-Very advanced communities live underwater and inside the Earth. They know who we are, what we do, and how long we have been living on the surface of the Earth. Some emerged in the past to teach early humans the art of speaking, writing and fishing.

8-Earth is the dumpster of the universe, home of the lowest human-life forms.

On earliest human species and our origin:
1-At the dawn of humanity, several human species had long tail.
2-An archaic human-reptilian race lived on planet Earth.
3-The modern human beings were genetically created by the Anunnaki.
4-The Anunnaki created us as humanoid-robots to serve their needs. We were "re-transformed" into humans following years of genetic manipulations.
5-Only a genetic manipulation of DNA sequences created the modern physiognomy of the human race, and stayed the very same for the past 11,000 years. The early form of humans was created some 65,000 years ago.
6-Neither the theory of Evolution nor the theory of the Creation is correct.

On the human mind and soul:
1-It is the vibrational projection of the cells in the human brain that lasts after death and is retransformed into another form of energy, not what we call the "Soul". Because soul as we think we know it does not exist; it is an idea created by early human beings for reasons not worthy discussing.

17

The Anunnaki Ulema said the very same thing. There is no soul trapped in the human body. This idea was created by the cave man even though he did not understand what soul is. It was his way to communicate with the "Divine" and the supernatural.

2-Humans have more than one brain in one location, although it is invisible to the naked eye. And the Enlightened Ones have a totally separate Mental Faculty (Mind, Fikr) in their "Conduit".

On UFOs:
Note: The words UFOs were never used in the meetings with aliens and extraterrestrials and the Aliens Transcripts. The words "Disc", and sometimes "Disk" were used instead.

UFOs' engines:
Some UFOs reactors (engines) use water as fuel, and no scientist on Earth could understand how these reactors function. The reactors were very small, impeccably clean, and without any "trace of combustion."

Metal memory:
Aliens' spacecrafts are made from several components; the most important one is "Metal Memory".

UFOs and time:
Since time is not linear, aliens can travel "Jump" into the future, and revisit the past simultaneously.
Intraterrestrials (The Grays) and extraterrestrials don't need special spacecrafts to do that.

UFOs crashes:
There is a total of 4 UFOs crashes on record; three in the United States, and one in Mexico. Two aliens who survived the crash were retained by the government.
The others were found dead, assumingly on impact.
From the two surviving aliens, one died after a few months; the other remained in U.S. custody for 6 months.

On the Grays "Greys":
The Grays concerns about our underground nuclear testing:

In 1992, the Grays met twice with civilian delegates, scientists and military men (Two Generals and one Lt. Colonel), in Arizona and Alaska. And they reached a final agreement, and a total/complete understanding that all underground testings should cease immediately.

As a result, the United States stopped undergound nuclear testings in 1992. Other leading countries followed suit. England's last nuclear testing occurred in 1991, Russia in 1990. France and China had a surprise-visit from the Grays in 1996. And before the end of 1996, both France and China abandonned their nuclear testings. In 1998, Pakistan and India were confronted by angry Grays, when both country detonnated their atomic bombs in the same year. And finally, the Pakistani and Indians got the message of the Grays.

On the Grays rewinding time and confusing abductees:
From an anthropologist and a military scientist:
The Grays purposely rewind time, past and future, to convince their abductees of their powers and intent to create a better world. The Grays have no sense of time.

However, they can clearly differentiate between past events and future events. They do not follow any chonological order or time-frame sequences when they project holographic images. Are they deliberately confusing their abductees? I don't think so.

Quite often, abductees are confused by the variety and speed of images they see on a holographic screen. It is not always the message, but the intent of the Grays that confuses them.

My personal opinion: It is not in the best interest of the Grays to confuse the abductees. The Grays have no intent to confuse the abductees, simply because, the abductees were already confused by the whole experience. Anybody would be confused, if he/she has been subjected to such an extraordinary event.

The confusion usually begins, as soon as the apparition of aliens occurs; long before, the Grays lift up, levitate, and abduct people. Most certainly, more confusions will follow up, when:
a-The abductees enter a spaceship out of this world,
b-The abductees are shown holographic images and footages;
c-Are directed to an operating room,
d-The aliens place them on a surgical bed,
e-The abductees see strange aliens operating on them.

f-The aliens show them the "Little Black Box".
All these sequences, events, and related phases of the abduction confuse the abductees. It is not exclusively the message or the speech of the aliens that confuse the abductees, but the whole process.

Time-space memory calendar:
The Grays have a time-space memory calendar that records all the events that occurred on Earth. The Anunnaki use the "Miraya" as a device to view past, present and future events.

Aliens' Corridor Plasma and the Vacuum Tunnel:
The Corridor Plasma is an underwater cold plasma tunnel temporarily (Periodically) created, used and transported by the intraterrestrials (The Grays) to navigate underwater.
It is undetectable by satellites or any sonar system. It functions via a web of 17 tunnels, called by the military "Channels" and "Tubes." The Corridor consists of a movable aquatic web of 17 underwater channels that links the aliens to their habitats, headquarters and communities. Starting in 1997, the web was referred to as the "Net", and the channels were called "Tubes".
Inquiring about the "Vacuum Tunnel", a scientist asked whether the tunnel can be measured, whether the tunnel is made from materials found on Earth, or whether the tunnel is created by the spacecraft itself, and could this tunnel be detected by us.
The alien answered that the tunnel could NOT be detected by us, or measured, because it is movable, temporarily used, it is not physical, and could not be detected by any sonar system.
Dr. Teller asked the alien about the "invisible" structure of the aliens' tunnel and what it consisted of.
The alien said, it is "Mitra" (Cold Plasma.)
I am absolutely sure that back then in mid 1948, none of our scientists understood or fully comprehended what a Cold Plasma was?! In 2010, I tried very modestly to explain this tunnel on the History Channel by describing it as "Corridor Plasma."

The Corridor Plasma was discussed numerous times in the Aliens Transcripts.
Corridor plasma is a term used to refer to underwater tunnels and passages created and operated by aliens to navigate the oceans.

By using these cold plasma tunnels, UFOs can accomplish extraordinary tasks, such as, to name a few:
- **a**- To reach an astonishing speed;
- **b**- To avoid sonar detection;
- **c**- To remain undetected by spy satellites;
- **d**- To enter and exit underwater bases.

The corridor plasma is movable and mobile, meaning that aliens can place the underwater tunnels, and displace them according to their needs, and "navigation chart".
The tunnels extend to thousands of miles underwater, and serve as a web network for several alien underwater bases around the globe.
Their spaceships known as USO (Unidentified Submerged Objects) use the plasma corridors to navigate the oceans and seas. According to some, the "Corridor Plasma can be compared to a White Hole, where gravity exists no longer.
In the White Holes, the gravity as we know it becomes a reverse gravity. This phenomenon allows the alien spacecrafts to attain a mind-boggling speed."
Some of these bases are located in:
- **a**- The Bahamas
- **b**- The Japanese "Dragon Triangle"
- **c**- The north side of the so-called Bermuda Triangle
- **d**- Alaska
- **e**- Florida
- The Grays intraterrestrials (Aliens who live on Earth) are the inventors of this astonishing technology.
- One of the most amazing aspects of this technology is the fact that the aliens' underwater crafts never touch the water.
- There is a plasma shield surrounding the exterior body of the craft. We know that plasma produces extreme heat. And this heat can melt the craft.
- But the aliens found a way to isolate the plasma heat from the body of the craft, by adding two layers of anti-plasma shields (Called Plasma Belt) to the exterior body of the craft.

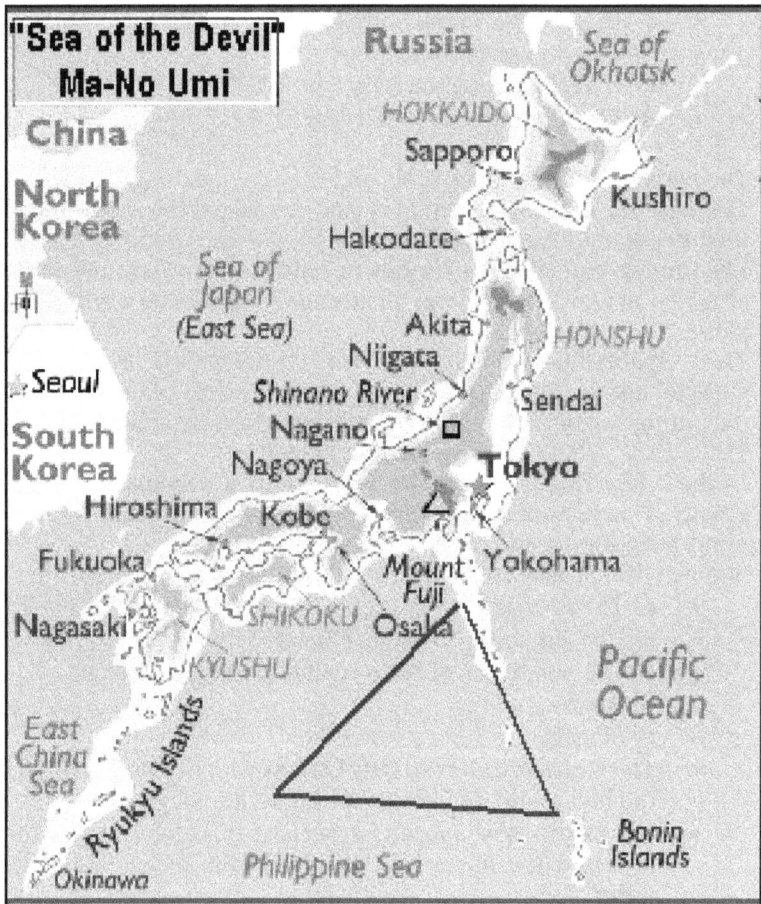

Map of the Japanese "Dragon Triangle".

Aquatic Plasma Corridors:
The Russians have a massive underwater base that was created in 1969, to study an extraterrestrial underwater navigation system called "Aquatic Plasma Corridors".
This corridor is undetectable by satellite, sonar or any other underwater detection system. Not all branches of the Russian Navy were aware of the creation/existence of this base.

Russians underwater encounter with aliens:
During one of their naval maneuvers just outside the perimeter of this Russian underwater base, six frogmen from one of the Russian submarines encountered three alien frogmen in metallic suits underneath a massive metallic object.
Both the Russian and alien frogmen were roughly at a depth of one hundred to one hundred and twenty feet.

The alien frogmen were wearing what appeared underwater, to be metallic suits of indeterminable and interchanging colors that morphed from a silvery white to bluish to grey.
One of the Russian frogmen stated that when he tried to approach these three, he was blocked by what seemed to be an invisible underwater force-field, created by the alien frogmen as a protection shield.

The Russian frogman's oxygen tanks started to fail and he quickly lost consciousness and started sinking but was saved by one of his fellow divers.
After being rescued, he described the alien frogmen as being 8ft to 11ft tall, as he saw them underwater. And none of them had any visible oxygen tanks/breathing apparatus attached to them.
In the secret debriefing that followed, the Russian diver who saved his fellow frogman, said that when he too tried to approach this massive foreign submerged object, he encountered what felt like a solid transparent wall surrounding the object. He later described it as an oval glass box, surrounding this mysterious submerged object which also shielded it from contact with the ocean's water.
After the fall of the Berlin wall, and ensuing collapse of the Soviet Empire, rumors started circulating within the military and scientific community, that this bizarre event was in fact a joint Russian-extraterrestrial operation designed to explore the effects

of the underwater plasma corridor on its environment in the ocean, and on humans, as well as their psychological and psychosomatic reactions to encountering the corridor and seeing the alien frogmen and the ship itself.

Two decades later in Lake Baikal, other Russian navy frogmen encountered similar 9ft "silver swimmers" who also had no visible breathing apparatus. While these encounters are largely unknown to the general public, military scientists with top clearance are well aware of them, and have worked on similar projects in different underwater bases in the United States.

Joint humans-aliens operations:
These massive underwater military bases, whether they are Russian, American or Chinese, they look from the surface as rectangular/traditional compound structures.

However upon entering them underwater, they expand in all directions, and are extremely extensive. And all of them are joint human-alien operations.

Starting from the second underwater level, compartments are divided into large operation rooms, separated by elaborate long corridors, curving at 90 degrees every hundred feet or so, with doors that can drop down from the ceiling to seal off segments in the event of radiation leakage, or any matter related to internal security.

One of the interesting characteristics of these doors in the corridors is the circular porthole-like windows within what is a whitish metal of an extraterrestrial origin.

None of these metallic alloys are possible here due to Earth's gravity, and as such have to be done in orbit aboard the Space Shuttle. Interestingly enough, this technology has been shared by American, Russian and Israeli military scientists.

At one time, British and French scientists complained of being left out of the loop, to which the Americans responded very candidly "We don't trust Europeans – especially the French!"

To which the French retorted that they would withhold all information garnered from the Cassini-Huygens mission to Saturn. An American three star general was quick to respond by saying "This is not the first time you Europeans have withheld information from us. Remember the Belgian incident?"

Mode of transportation down to the underwater base:
The mode of transportation down to the underwater base and within the base is also fascinating.

From the surface, one enters a craft that looks like a silvery metallic spinning top, approximately 8ft in diameter, that can comfortably accommodate four passengers, and corkscrews its way downwards centrifugally around a rod using a form of magnetic propulsion for what seems to be a only a few seconds down to an unknown depth.

From the second underwater level on down, the "Spinning Mobile Satellite" (SMS) travels horizontally and reaches its final destination at an undisclosed level of the base at which it again dives into water. It is at that level/destination that you will find the habitat and work center of the Grays. (Previously mentioned)

The Radio Plasma Belt (RPB):
A report referred to the RPB, created by the intraterrestrials to isolate earth from the universe. This belt can expand up or down, and can affect missiles, rockets, or airplanes, and blow them up. It explains what has happened to various airplanes in Vietnam, and also to human spacecrafts and space missions.

Alien cybernetic organism (ACO): A theory on the Greys advanced by John Lear, who stated that there are several types of aliens-Greys.

Mr. Lear said, "The Greys are not a species themselves. They work for a higher authority, and they are programmed...some have 4 fingers with no thumb, some have 3 fingers, some 6 fingers. Some have no toes at all, but have sock-life feet..."

Alien frogmen: The Russians have a massive underwater base that was created in 1969, to study an extraterrestrial underwater navigation system called "Aquatic Plasma Corridors".

This corridor is undetectable by satellite, sonar or any other underwater detection system. Not all branches of the Russian Navy were aware of the creation/existence of this base.

During one of their naval maneuvers just outside the perimeter of this Russian underwater base, six frogmen from one of the Russian submarines encountered three alien frogmen in metallic suits underneath a massive metallic object.

Both the Russian and alien frogmen were roughly at a depth of one hundred to one hundred and twenty feet.

The alien frogmen were 8ft to 11ft tall:

The alien frogmen were wearing what appeared underwater to be metallic suits of indeterminable and interchanging colors that morphed from a silvery white to bluish to grey. One of the Russian frogmen stated that when he tried to approach these three, he was blocked by what seemed to be an invisible underwater force-field, created by the alien frogmen as a protection shield.

The Russian frogman's oxygen tanks started to fail and he quickly lost consciousness and started sinking but was saved by one of his fellow divers.

After being rescued, he described the alien frogmen as being 8ft to 11ft tall, as he saw them underwater. And none of them had any visible oxygen tanks/breathing apparatus attached to them.

In the secret debriefing that followed, the Russian diver who saved his fellow frogmen, said that when he too tried to approach this massive foreign submerged object, he encountered what felt like a solid transparent wall surrounding the object.

An oval glass box surrounded and shielded the aliens' underwater craft.

He later described it as an oval glass box, surrounding this mysterious submerged object which also shielded it from contact with the ocean's water. After the fall of the Berlin wall, and ensuing collapse of the Soviet Empire, rumors started circulating within the military and scientific community, that this bizarre event was in fact a joint Russian-extraterrestrial operation designed to explore the effects of the underwater plasma corridor on it's environment in the ocean, and on humans, as well as their psychological and psychosomatic reaction to encountering the corridor and seeing the alien frogmen and the ship itself.

Two decades later in Lake Baikal, other Russian navy frogmen encountered similar 9ft "silver swimmers" who also had no visible breathing apparatus.

While these encounters are largely unknown to the general public, military scientists with top clearance are well aware of them, and have worked on similar projects in different underwater bases, such as the one known to us as AUTEC, which is located off Andros Island in the Bahamas.

Massive underwater bases.
These massive underwater military bases, whether they be Russian, or American or Chinese, look from the surface to be rectangular/traditional compound structures.
However upon entering them underwater, they expand in all directions, and are extremely extensive. And all of them are joint human-alien operations.
Starting from the second underwater level, compartments are divided into large operation rooms, separated by elaborate long corridors, curving at 90 degrees every hundred feet or so, with doors that can drop down from the ceiling to seal off segments in the event of radiation leakage, or any matter related to internal security.

One of the interesting characteristics of these doors in the corridors is the circular porthole-like windows within what is a whitish metal of extraterrestrial origin.
None of these metallic alloys are possible here due to earth's gravity, and as such have to be done in orbit aboard the Space Shuttle. Interestingly enough, this technology has been shared by American, Russian and Israeli military scientists.

Aliens' Black Box: For many years, and in numerous countries, a great number of abductees reported on a mysterious and macabre "Alien Black Box".
Allegedly, it is a little black box, the alien abductors, (in some unspecified instances) show to abductees, point to it, and return to their spacecraft. It seems bizarre, but unfortunately it did happen, according to very reliable contactees and abductees.
Many abductees, including experiencers wondered what was the meaning of all this? Why the extraterrestrials did not explain to them the reason for showing them this box? Well, they did, but abductees did not get it.
Allegedly, the little black box contains a live fetus of a hybrid entity (creature), which is part human and part alien Gray.
The aliens show the Black Box to their abductees, and point them to a small entity which resembles human beings; sometime, they are babies, and some other time, adult (Males and females).

The aliens don't say a word. They just open the box and display its content. The intention of the aliens is clear: Look and see how we can duplicate you and create your replacement!

What the abductees see is essentially a holographic photo of their children; children they will give birth to, when impregnated artificially in the aliens' test-tubes.

Simply put, the Grays are developing a new human race; a race called Grays-Humans Hybrids.

Aliens' rapture:

I. Definition and introduction: The aliens' rapture (AR) is part confrontation/collision, and part separation.

Although extraterrestrials are highly advanced, their high level of technology and baffling scientific knowledge are not categorically a code for morality and ethics.

Science, whether on planet Earth or beyond, can be used for ill purposes. Such possibility exists all over the universe.

Thus, frictions, confrontations, oppositions, separation, and wars on the galactic landscape of extraterrestrials happen on a regular basis.

In fact, the very first time, humans have heard of visitors from outer space, was through depictions of aliens' destruction of cities on Earth, and wars between God and the Fallen Angels, and between the Nephilim, the Biblical Giants, the Watchers, the Guardians, the Legions of Darkness, and the Shining Ones, in the Bible, in the holy scriptures, in the banned books from the Bible, in the Gnostic scrolls, and ancient Mesopotamian clay tablets. And all them were of an extraterrestrial stock!

Aliens' destruction of cities, burning people alive, and turning humans into pillars of salt were neither promising, nor reassuring for humankind.

So yes, extraterrestrials can fight each other, as we do often here on Earth. And Nikola Tesla was very concerned.

II. Do we have any authoritative source(s) on the aliens' rapture and extraterrestrials' communications?

There are obscure, authoritative and very few sources that tell us something about the aliens' rapture, its origin, past or current development, and how it could affect the present and future of humanity.

These sources also reveal baffling governmental "notes", and top secret memoranda on extraterrestrials' communications between two (or more) alien spaceships.

Some of these sources are:
a-The Anunnaki-Ulema.
b-The Book of Ramadosh.
c-Statements by Anunnaki-Human-Hybrids.
d-Statements by two highly respected astronomers, currently teaching at leading American universities, and working at some of the world's most advanced observatories. Their names will not be released, even though, they gave statements on the History Channel and the Science Channel in the United States, in 2008.
e-Opinions of bona fide scientists (Astrophysicists, cosmologists and astronomers) who worked at SETI, for a very long time.
Their names will not be released, even though, they gave their statements in open discussions, and on the History Channel and the Science Channel in the United States, in 2008.
f-Opinions and claims of eminent scientists and professors at Moscow Academy of Medicine (Moscow Sechenov Academy of Medicine), given in 1987, and in 1988.
Their names will not be released, as long as, they are still teaching at the academy.
g-World War Two's famous cryptologists who worked on the German Enigma Machine codes, deciphering machines, and teleprinters, previously located in Room 40 of the British Admiralty Building, an undisclosed unit of Britain's military intelligence.
In 1957, they explained how the British in 1956 and in 1959, tried to decipher some extraterrestrial messages. For national security reasons, their names shall not be released.
h-Nikola Tesla's papers: There is no doubt, Nikola Tesla who was in touch with Maria Orsic knew a lot about the extraterrestrial phenomenon. Sava Kosanovic reported that his uncle Nikola Tesla told him about the German Bell-UFO, and Maria Orsic's Vril, and in one of his correspondences with Marshal Tito, he explained to the Yugoslavian leader how these machines could work.

The personal files of Nikola Tesla, seized by the United States government, right after his death in 1943, revealed beyond the shadow of doubt, that:
a-UFOs are real.
b-There are many planets inhabited by intelligent civilizations,
c-A contact with extraterrestrials is possible, if we have adequate instruments.
d-Some galactic civilizations are in constant confrontation with other civilizations, and are part of the aliens' cosmic rapture.

Extraterrestrials' warning: From reading Nicola Tesla's files, some of the United States military scientists concluded that the extraterrestrials are fighting each other, and some alien species are already here on Earth, preparing for a major confrontation. What kind of confrontation?
Nobody knew at the time.
However, in a third meeting with the aliens, the United States military learned that "Gray Alien" species living underwater, and in an adjacent dimension, will confront the Americans, unless an agreement is reached between the aliens and the United States government.
The aliens did in fact refer to an "Alien Rapture" that has occurred under the nose of a "Galactic Extraterrestrial Council", commonly known in ufology's literature as the "Federation".
See Tesla.

Alien reproduction vehicles (ARV): A technical term for replicas of extraterrestrials spaceships, and terrestrial-galactic crafts designed and manufactured by American avionics and aerospace companies for the United States government. The most notable manufacturers are Northrup, Lockheed Martin, SAIC, and E-Systems.

Alien spacecraft simulator (ASS): A technical term for a man-made machine with a simulator mounted above a circular pit of 38 feet in diameter, and approximately 21 feet in width. An insider has claimed that the simulator is a fully operational flying saucers.

Aliens-US Dulce base, the:

We have two reports on Dulce base from Sinhar Ambar Ana.Ti, (Ana-Noura) and Marjana; two women who were acknowledged to be Anunnaki offspring.

The Anbar Ana. Ti account:

It was reported by Ambar Anati, a hybrid-alien, of an Anunnaki origin, that she spent many years in the United States, and attended NYU. The story was told in a biography of Anati, I co-wrote with the distinguished Dr. Anbel.

To many, Anati's account on how she met with the CIA and NSA agents in Washington, DC, her flight to a US Air Force base, her visit to Dulce underground base, her meetings with the Grays, and how she burned down the base is a pure fantasy.

To others, a possibility. And to a few, the real McCoy. You will be the judge.

Anati in her own words: I went to a hotel in New York. I had with me a special device, an ingenious thing that had on it the special telephone numbers of top members of the National Security Agency, or NSA as everyone refers to them.

Only two or three people in the world have these numbers, not even the president of the United States has access to them. They are used only for matters related to extraterrestrial reverse engineering.

The device makes sure the phones will be promptly answered, and when I called, I gave them data that they recognized as their own extra terrestrial material.

They were shocked, but nevertheless they agree to meet with me. I suppose they realized they had no choice. Rather politely, they offered to fly me to Washington DC, where they wanted to have the meeting, but I informed them that it was not necessary.

It was easy for me to simply materialize in DC, and I did not want them to know my current address, if this could be prevented. They directed me to come to the Four Seasons hotel in Georgetown, where they were to meet me at the lobby.

I was to know, if questioned at the hotel, that I was heading for the suite that was reserved under the name of a Middle Eastern gentleman who owned a limousine service in DC, and had often used the hotel for similar purposes.

I materialized a little distance away from the hotel, and walked there on M Street. Three members of the NSA were waiting for me, and they took me to the reserved suite, where fifteen more people were sitting around a huge table.

They rose and greeted me politely, but I could clearly see the suspicion in their eyes and in their thoughts. I noticed that the shades of all the windows were closed, and I saw no telephones.

However, they all had gadgets in their hands which I have recognized immediately. They were navigation devices, which at the time were known only to extraterrestrials, not to any humans. For a moment I assumed that they got it from the Grays, for communication purposes, and then noticed that quite a few of these people were really Grays who had shape-shifted to resemble humans.

I can easily identify them, because even while shape-shifting, the Grays cannot turn their heads independently of their body. They have to turn the entire body if they wish to look to the sides. As they turn, their eyes cannot follow their heads quickly, like humans' eyes, but they have to refocus. All that is done rather discretely, but after living with the Hybrids and the Grays, I could not miss that.

In addition, humans usually fidget, move around. The Grays never do. When seated, they sit quietly, immobile. When standing, they are straight and immobile as well. In addition to that, I had more instructions from Nibiru as to how to recognize all shape-shifters, which I cannot explain because it involves using the Conduit.

One of the Grays at the end of the table was tapping nervously on the edge of the table with something that looked like a pen, and from time to time pointed it towards me. I recognized this gadget as a scanning device, such as we use on Ashtari (Aldebaran).

It was not held by any of the humans, because this fiber/scanning device was not known to the humans' scientific community until much later, 2006 or 2007.

I supposed the Grays kept it to themselves for a while. I did my best to ignore the fact that half the people there were Grays, and proceeded as if I had no idea and was talking only to humans.

I had nothing to fear, really, since I could annihilate the Grays with one thought, and I decided that discretion was the best approach. The Grays maintained their pretence throughout it, and I said nothing at all.

Come to think of it, I was used to the treachery of the Grays, but I have to admit I was a little distressed by the humans' duplicity and stupidity.

Did they really think I won't recognize the Grays?

I have explained to them who I was, telling the absolute truth, and giving my name as Ambar Anati. Naturally they did not believe me. To help persuade them, I first of all, projected certain images on one of the walls.

These were holographic pictures that showed them the entire sequence of the Roswell crash, where the Gray was held, and data pertaining to their research.

They still were not persuaded that I was who I claimed to be, but the fact that the projections were done without any equipment made them uneasy and less sure of themselves. They were at least ready to listen. I told them quite a lot about the Grays and their agenda. "By now," I said, "you must be aware that they do not tell the truth, that they are not to be trusted."

"Business is business," said one of them. "They have given us more than they promised, too, so we have gained additional knowledge. It's not really a big deal if they abduct a few more people."

"First of all, it is not a few people. It's thousands that are tortured and killed."

"What can we say?" answered another.

Sometimes harsh measures cannot be avoided." I did my best to hide my feelings about such a statement, and went on.

"Are you aware of the fact that they are trying to take over earth?"

"No, we were not informed about such intent," said another.

"And are you aware of the invisible radio plasma belt around earth?

They want to isolate earth from the universe. This belt can expand up or down, and can affect missiles, rockets, or airplanes, and blow them up. It explains what has happened to various airplanes in Vietnam, and also to human spacecrafts and space missions."

"We don't understand what you want us to do," said one of them.

"I want you to trust the Anunnaki. They intend to help you get rid of the Grays. This is really very simple. Either you go with the Anunnaki, in which case much can be done, or you stay with the Grays. If you choose to stay with the Grays, the Anunnaki will return and clean up the earth, in a way that you will not like.

They are perfectly capable of annihilating the entire population if the atrocities do not stop."

"Are you threatening us?" asked one of them. The rest stared at me, impassive.

"I would not call it a threat," I said. "I would call it a fair warning. Remember, the Anunnaki are stronger than both humans and Grays.

They did not have to send me, they could do what they wanted without warning. But they prefer to save as many humans as possible."

"How do we know how strong the Anunnaki really are?" said one of them. "After all, they have been away for so long. They don't seem to have much of an interest in us."

"Let me show you a small example of what the Anunnaki can do," I said.

In a blink, I multiplied myself into thirty copies; we arranged ourselves around the table, behind the sitting people. They jumped off their seats, shocked.

"It's a trick," cried some of them. "Grab her!"

"Please, do grab," I said. "Touch all thirty of me, and see that this is not an idle trick. We can become billions, if we wish." Hesitantly, they touched some of the multiples. A few multiples offered to shake hands, which the humans did, trembling. They could not deny the multiple's tangible presence.

I contracted myself into one person again, and sat down. "Please," I said.

"I have no desire to frighten you. Sit down and let's be reasonable."

"Truth is, said one of them, "The Grays are an immediate threat. They are right here and we cannot control them. The Anunnaki are far away. But still, we can see that you wish to help us, and it should be considered. What would you want us to do?"

My visit to the Dulce underground base.

"I want to start by going into some of the more important places where humans and Grays interact," I said. "I need much data to deliver to the High Council of Ashtari and receive instructions before I meet the President of the United States, among others."

"I think the best thing to do is to go to Dulce, in New Mexico. It is the most important joint laboratory of the Grays and the U.S. Government," said one of them. The others nodded in agreement.

"There are bases in Nevada, Arizona, and Colorado, among others, but Dulce is the most important."

"Very well. Would you assign one of the members to come with me, act as my escort?" I asked.

"Yes, Colonel X— will go with you." The colonel rose. He seemed to be a respectable, middle-aged man. In reality, he was certainly a Gray. As before, I pretended not to notice.

"Would you like me to materialize you there?" I asked.

"No, I think it's best if we go in a more traditional way," said the colonel. "We don't want to startle the People in Dulce too much. It's best if they don't panic." I agreed and we decided to go the next day, in a military plane.

On the plane, the colonel, who had become reasonably friendly, gave me some information about Dulce.

"It's all underground, you know" he said. "People know about seven layers, but in truth, there are nine I am aware of, perhaps more I don't even know about. It's really a very large compound."

"Where exactly is it?" I asked.

"It lies under Archuleta Mesa on the Jicarilla Apache Indian Reservation, near the town of Dulce.

Very easy to keep it a secret, the way it is constructed," he said. "And they are very careful about security. You will see."

We finally landed at the small air field. A not medium sized building, guarded and surrounded with a high wire fence, stood in the desert.

We entered a normal room. I noticed the cameras in the entrance, and a woman in military uniform looked at some papers Colonel Jones presented to her, but the security was not impressive.

I realized later that the deeper you went into the compound, the stricter was the security. She pressed a button, and a man came to escort us through a door that led to an escalator.

From then on, it seemed we were descending into Hell. Everything was clean, shiny, and metallic, much like I remembered from my unpleasant stay with the Hybrids. No matter where you looked, you saw a security camera. There were side doors everywhere.

Apparently, many secret exits and entrances existed, and each was loaded with security features, some seen, some invisible. On the first level we were joined by a Gray. He was polite and distant, and showed us into various offices without much comment.

The offices were normal, military, and stark. Maps hung on walls, with many pushpins in various colors stuck into them. The individual colors, the Gray explained, showed sites of high activity of different subjects.

Green, for example, showed sites of heavy spaceship activities, including those of extraterrestrials that were not Grays, and were considered enemies by them.

Red were for areas of cattle mutilation and collection of animal blood. Blue indicated underground activities and caverns. I do not remember all the other colors and sites, but the arrangement was quite elaborate.

The offices were monitored constantly by humans, who wore military-like jumpsuits. Each carried a gun, quite visibly.

All the uniforms were decorated with the symbol of the Triangle, much like the Phoenician symbol. They had various letters in each triangle, supposedly signifying rank, but I never found out if this was true. When they saw that we were accompanied by the Gray, they simply ignored us.

The second level was exactly the same, full of offices, but after the first level, which we reached by the escalator, we used only elevators. I was told that the elevators had no cables in them, and were controlled magnetically, using alien technology. Magnetism also supplied light, which came from flat, round objects, and there were no regular light bulbs in sight.

The third level was devoted to hospital-like environment used for impregnation of female humans.

I was not allowed into the surgical ward itself, but the Gray explained that the experimenters removed the fetus, and placed it for speeded-up growth in an incubator, creating Hybrids.

In this facility, more than in the one I visited during my previous time with the hybrids, they tended to experiment with genetic manipulation during the very early time in the incubator.

The results were quite monstrous sometimes.

Through windows in the walls, I saw cribs, or really a sort of cages, with some of the results. Deformed humans were the norm – extra arms and legs, small or very large heads, and creatures that did not really look humans. "What do you do with these?" I asked.

"We harvest certain tissues and then kill them," said the Gray. "We learn quite a lot from them about genetics. We apply them to our own research."

On level four, there were genetic labs that created half human/half animals. Their shapes, as I saw them sitting in their cages, were so horrific, that I had to avert my eyes. Some of them had a reptilian look, some had fur, and others looked like gargoyles. "Do you harvest tissues here too?" I asked.

"Yes, we combine this research with the materials we get from the cows. The research is extremely interesting and useful," said the Gray.

The aliens had their living quarters on levels five, six, and seven. These looked much like military barracks, as we passed the corridors and peeked into the rooms, but I saw no reason to enter.

I asked the Gray if it was true that there were additional levels. This did not seem to phase him at all, and he said, in his perfect English that seemed so unpleasant, coupled with his scratchy alien voice, that yes, of course.

Apparently, they took advantage of the huge natural caverns under Dulce, and created additional levels.

They carried even more security there, and the Gray said that if we wanted to go there, he would have to call two more Grays to accompany us, and we would need to use an eye identification system. These details were quickly accomplished, and we used a side elevator to the eighth level. Here they also experimented with manipulation of the nervous system by various means. It allowed them to cause disease and even death from a distance.

"I am afraid you cannot enter the place where the subjects are kept," said the Gray.

"These subjects are mostly insane, dangerous, and very susceptible to changes in the routine. If we enter, we might destroy some of the experiments."

Level nine, where we were invited to enter, contained storage of fully grown creatures and tissues in vats, all dead. This included tanks full of embryos in various stages of development, weighting for use. The place was kept as clean as the rest of the compound, but the smell of the chemicals was overwhelming.

I simply could not stay there long, and Colonel Jones, who until that time showed no emotion, suddenly shape-shifted and appeared in his real, Gray form.

"You knew all along, Ms. Anati," he said, his voice turning scratchy.

"I never thought we could trick you, and would have preferred to appear in my true form in the first place, but my group insisted."

"It does not signify," I said. "Of course I knew."

The other Gray did not pay much attention to the shifting, being used to such practices.

Level ten, the most secret of them all, was devoted to human aura research, and other extra sensory abilities, including dreams, hypnosis, etc. The researchers were able to record dreams on specialized machines; the dreams were studied as part of the major advanced study of psychic power and phenomena.

"Once we are more advanced in this research," said the Gray, "we will have total power over other races. Of course, we mean no harm to humans nor to the Anunnaki. We are merely concerned with the Reptilian races."

I almost laughed. No harm to humans? Was the Gray trying to be a PR person?

When we finished our tour, we were escorted out of the complex. The plane waited for us outside. I said nothing about my disgust, horror, and disbelief to anyone.

But I have seen enough, and I knew that this was just the tip of the iceberg. Such treaties must have been entered into by more than the United States government. The Grays have reached almost total control over humanity.

After materializing myself back to New York, I knew I will always be watched, but I also knew how to handle it and avoid my watchers. I needed time.

First, I spent a few days just digesting what I saw. I made myself invisible, and left the hotel for hours of exploration.

I walked the streets, took the subway, went on buses, and visited museums, stores, offices, hospitals, senior citizens home, schools, and more. Everywhere I went I saw Grays in shape-shifted form. Obviously, they did not only infiltrate the military, but spread out much more. They flooded the city.

Some worked in offices, some in restaurants, obviously doing it as part of their agenda.

They were nurses, teachers, officials, sanitation engineers. They were probably doing the same in other cities, urban areas, towns, and even other countries. For me, as I mentioned before, it is easy to recognize a shape-shifter.

I was taught how to do it by the best teachers on Ashtari. But a human cannot do so very easily. Your doctor could be one. The nice lady in the department store could be one.
The teacher of your young child could be one. In addition, I saw many hybrids. Vicious, unfeeling, and manipulative, they flocked mostly into the entertainment industry, the financial world, and the advertising field. It seemed they liked glamour. The Grays and their slaves, the Hybrids, have invaded the world.
After a few days I got to work. Using the same device that had gotten me the telephone numbers of the NSA members, I spent my time contacting and negotiating with hundreds of people from a number of governments on earth.
I also visited other laboratories, bases, and Air Force fields. Each time I negotiated, I have encountered the same road blocks.
Every government on earth was in terror of the Grays. The Anunnaki were feared, too, and the knowledge that they will very likely attempt to clean the earth, terrified the humans, but not enough to get them out of their fearful paralysis regarding the Grays.

Anunnaki Marjana's account, as directly provided by Robert Dr. Hutton.
From the meeting with the Americans, to Dulce Base visit.
Some characters and personages' names are altered to protect their identity.

Marjana's meeting at the Pentagon.
Day and Time: Thursday 10:00 AM.
Present at the meeting (Names altered):
General Hutchinson, DOD (United States Department of Defense) presiding
General Harry McMullen, San Antonio Air Materiel, Kelly Air Force Base, San Antonio, Texas.
General Nathan F. Kenney, United States Air Force Chief of Staff
General Ramsey, DOD
General Arnold, USSTRATCOM (U.S. Strategic Command)
Colonel Goldmark, Army Research and Development Command
Director of the CIA
Dr. Robert Hutton
Dr. Samuelson

Dr. Aaron Berger
Four scientists and two physicians (One pathologist, and one neurologist From Walter Reed Military Medical Center)
Four cameramen
A sergeant in charge of recording the meeting
Two agents from the NSA
A strange looking observer (Later identified as a Gray-Hybrid)
A very important code breaker, who previously worked with Alan Turing, at Huts 1, 3, 6, where cryptology was conducted at Bletchley Park in England, during World War Two
A psychologist
A prominent linguist from Georgetown University
A university professor from Berkeley
Two scientists from NASA
A Noble Prize winner in Physics
A military man operating a speaking/communication device
A military man operating a recording device
Two military technicians handling projectors
A military RN (She was present at two previous meetings with other aliens. Never to be seen again)
A highly decorated military pilot, working at Area 51
Two unidentified persons (They never said a word)
An unidentified person, possibly from India or Burma.
Twenty fully armed soldiers
Five MPs
All are seated around a huge crescent-shape table, except:
Cameramen positioned at the very end of the room,
A nurse and two paramedic (s) standing nearby some sort of medical equipments
A typist seated at the other end of the room, and facing the emergency exit,
A tough-looking sergeant in charge of recording the meeting, seated behind a large desk, on the opposite direction of the cameramen,
Four military men behind projectors positioned at different angles at each corner of the room,
Twenty fully armed soldiers standing against the walls of the room with an order of shoot to kill; an order given by the Joint Chief of Staff.

The meeting room looks like a war zone, only tanks and jets are missing. In front of where General Hutchinson is seated (at the very middle of the table), and at an approximate distance of fifteen feet from the table, an elevated base of two feet in height, and four feet by five feet in dimension, could not be missed; the base is especially constructed for the occasion, and where Riya-Marjana will be asked to stand on.

The base is separated from the table by a thick fiberglass divider (Box) on three sides, designed to prevent any possible radio-active emission's leak from the body of the alien or contagious germs, which could harm the attendees.
The box has the appearance of a transparent cage and which very greatly offends Riya-Marjana, as the fiberglass divider begins to rise from under the carpet to reach a height of eight feet.
When the light projectors are spotted directly at the base, the area where Riya-Marjana is supposed to stand on, looks like an electrical chair steaming in an execution room.
It is a horrifying scene. Everything looks like a macabre circus.

Behind the glass cage, two bizarre looking concave mirrors are strategically positioned at 45 degree, so everybody could see everything happening behind Riya-Marjana's back.
At the very end of the room, and behind a thick black velvet curtain, two stretchers are concealed, in case the alien is shut and/or needs urgent medical attention.

Next to stretchers, two sets of oxygen tanks are visible, and which add more drama and theatrics to the whole scene. It is disgusting and repulsive to say the least.
All of a sudden, all lights are shut off for unknown reasons, and the room plunges into an abyss of darkness for 5 long seconds.
Attendees are concerned, and become agitated.

General Hutchinson: What is going on, in here?
(Talking to a Lt. Commander, his military aide)
Jay, go find out what...
But before finishing his sentence, a strong light bursts inside the room exactly where Riya-Marjana is supposed to stand; she suddenly appears from nowhere.

The lights come back, everybody is relieved for a second or two, but a new fear mirrors over their faces as Riya-Marjana materializes in front of them, in the flesh and out of the blue.

General Hutchinson: Dr. Hutton...could you explain what is happening here? Is this your alien?

Dr. Robert Hutton: Yes sir. This is Marjana. This is how usually Anunnaki make their appearance. There is no danger, General.

General Hutchinson (Talking to Riya-Marjana): Quite an entrance you made! What's the meaning of all this?

General Ramsey: Welcome...Welcome indeed!

Silence. No answer from Marjana. Obviously she is upset by the spectacle of the fiberglass cage rising from under her feet.

General Ramsey (Asking Dr. Hutton): Why doesn't she answer?

Dr. Robert Hutton: Give her a few seconds, General.

(Talking to Marjana). Hi Riya! Happy to see you! This is General Ramsey, and there, General Hutchinson, he is in charge of the meeting.

Again, no answer from Marjana.

Dr. Robert Hutton: Something wrong Marjana? Are you OK?

Still, no answer from Marjana. Suddenly she says something to Robert in Ana'kh. Nobody understands a word.

Marjana: Irfa faslou Ma ragbi

General Hutchinson: What did she say? What did she tell you?

Dr. Robert Hutton: She wants you to get rid of the cage, General. She is upset.

General Hutchinson: I can't do that, I don't know what she is up to?

Dr. Robert Hutton: Sir, if you don't, she will...without even touching it. Please General.

General Hutchinson gives the order to lower down the cage.

Marjana: That's better. Much better.

General Hutchinson: Ahhhhh.... You speak English!

Marjana: Better than you think.

General Hutchinson: OK...let's start from the beginning. What's your name?

Marjana: Riyah-Marjana.

General Ramsey: I am General Hutchinson from the United States Air Force.

Marjana: I know who you are. You studied at West Point. You're are Presbyterian and divorced twice. You're alcoholic.

You smoke cheap cigars. You cheat when you play cards...And your screen stinks!
General Ramsey laughing. Laughs in the background.
General Hutchinson: And you are the Holy Spirit! Frankly, I don't know who you are lady.
Marjana: I am Riya-Marjana, the official envoy of the Anunnaki Council.
General Ramsey: No offense meant.
General Hutchinson: How did you know I am alcoholic.... divorced twice...and
Marjana (Interrupting): We have been monitoring your military bases, your progress, your government, your generals, and you are no exception.
General Hutchinson: I see. You said...your are the official envoy of the Anunnaki. I see you alone, without a delegation, no...
Marjana (Interrupting): Pull the curtains and look outside.
General Hutchinson leaves his seat, goes straight to the inside right wall, pushes the curtain aside and looks from the window.
An immense spacecraft is hovering over The Pentagon.
He is baffled.
General Hutchinson: Is this your spacecraft?
General Ramsey rushes to the window and sees the spacecraft.
Marjana: Look again.
General Hutchinson: It's gone!
Marjana: Look again.
General Ramsey: It's back!
General Hutchinson (Looking again at the spacecraft): It's gone!
Marjana: This is my delegation. Are you satisfied?
General Hutchinson and General Ramsey return to their seats.
General Hutchinson: Where did you come from?
Marjana: Ashtari.
General Arnold: Where is Ashtari?
Marjana: You call it Aldebaran...Alpha Tauri.
General Hutchinson: What do they call you on Alpha Tauri?
Marjana: It depends where I am, and whom I am visiting.
General Ramsey: Would you care to explain, please?
Marjana: We do not call each other by name, unless it is absolutely necessary...and only if we are at Ashtari our home planet. In many parts of where we live, there is no atmosphere...

And where there is no atmosphere there, is no air. And where there is no air...no sounds are heard.

General Ramsey: I see. So... how do you breathe?

Marjana: We don't need air and we don't need oxygen to breathe. We generate our own energy from our inner organism.

Dr. Robert Hutton: The Anunnaki have a cell in their brain called Fik'r. It provides all the necessary energy they need to animate their body and activate their brain. They breathe through their mind. They don't need lungs or a respiratory system.

Dr. Samuelson: Are you built the same as us?

Marjana: We don't have your lungs. We don't have your abdomen. We don't eat the way you do. We don't have a digestive system. And we don't produce wastes. We don't feel pain because we don't have a nervous system. We don't express ourselves with physical emotions.

Dr. Aaron Berger: If you don't have emotions, how do you express yourselves?

Marjana: Our emotions are not physical, they are mental. You live in a physical world...We live in time-space dimension.

General Ramsey: What does that mean?

Marjana: Even if I explained it to you, you wouldn't understand.

Dr. Samuelson: Our brain operates our physical body, how do you operate yours? What makes your body function? Muscles, brains, a program?

Marjana: I can function without my body. I can duplicate myself.

Dr. Aaron Berger: A new body?

Marjana: Yes, and you would not notice the difference.

Dr. Robert Hutton: She meant, the body is just a façade. Each copy is a duplicate of a façade, or a previous copy.

Dr. Aaron Berger: In other words, it is shape-shifting?

Marjana: You mean like that?

And suddenly, Marjana starts to shape-shift...changing her face from a woman to the face of President Lincoln, to the face of President George Washington, to the face of Andrew Jackson, to the face of an eagle, to a ball of light...and back to her face.

Everybody was terrified!

Marjana: I can't stay much longer. But I would like to meet with you very soon. I have a message for you...and I want to talk to you about Earth's future, the Anunnaki Council's concerns, your and why I am here.

General Ramsey: Absolutely. We will arrange more meetings with Dr. Hutton. Will you be around?
Marjana: Only for a short time.

And suddenly, Marjana vanishes in a thin air, leaving behind her an exquisite fragrance...the aroma of a celestial woman who transcends time and space with her supernatural powers and eternal beauty.

Marjana's second meeting at area 51.
Building "S2". Time: 11:00 AM.
Security is intense. MPs are everywhere. More than 50 guards armed to the teeth surround Building "S2", where the meeting is taking place. The area is deserted. Not a soul.
It looks like a phantom town.
Not a single car in the parking lot, except 5 jeeps parked in front of Building "S2". All flights to and from Area 51 are cancelled.
Two large transport/cargo airplanes are grounded at the end of a runway. A civilian passengers' plane known as "Janet" which daily transports employees to Area 51 is seen at the very end of runway 2. The only thing moving are the security cameras and a strong swirling wind covering empty buildings with a grayish dust and waves of a steamy fog. Because of this significant and above top secret meeting, civilians, engineers and aliens working at Area 51 are transferred to another facility.
Marjana and Dr. Robert Hutton are inside a tiny reception room in Building "S2". They are arguing. They have been waiting for half an hour. Dr. Robert Hitton seems anxious, while Marjana is totally relaxed. Strangely enough, she looks now, much much taller, almost 6 feet 7 inches.
Dr. Robert Hutton: Any reason for doubling your size? You are already a giant!
Marjana: I know what I am doing.
Dr. Robert Hutton: Still, I can't believe it! I am looking at an alien? An Anunnaki woman. Practically, I am living with one.
Marjana: How many times did I tell you not to use this word?
Dr. Robert Hutton: But you are an alien! Aren't you?
Marjana: You are alien too... to billions of civilizations. And the way you look scares the hell out of them!

45

_____

Dr. Robert Hutton: Really?? You told me yourself, aliens are scary...They don't have eyes, they don't have ears, no hands, no lungs and no body's organs...they are useless to them. They are frightening biological machines with three fingers! I don't find this very pretty. It is horrifying!

Marjana: Horrifying to you...not to billions of highly advanced civilizations. They are just different.

Eyes like yours are not needed in outer space...they use different organs to see...some use skins pores, others cells in the brain.

And the brain is not necessary located inside a skull; it could be found anywhere under the skin, or on the surface. Nothing wrong with that. Nothing horrifying at all. Your people are doing the same thing.

They created half humans-half machines...Prefabricated hands and feet, robots without soul, without lungs and without heart.

We know what is going on at Walt Disney studios! And all these hideous creatures you mass produced, and copied from Derinkuyu and Gobekli Tepe. And how about those awful Type BE hybrids you created with the Ardi-Nishtaar? They are all over New York, Washington and Nevada! Ask your friend General Ramsey about the Black Conic Box. Ask him about the Compressor... The BCB and Adenosine Triphosphate, the ERW...the AGM-114N...The Plastic Neutron Bomb.

Dr. Robert Hutton: Take it easy, will you? Slow down. How did you know about all this?

Marjana: We used the Miraya. We monitor everything you do.

How your Ardi-Nishtaar friends abduct people...what they do to them at Dulce Base with full consent of your government. I am taking you there as soon as I finish my business here. I will show you the horrors of your government and of the Ardi-Nishtaar on the Miraya...They (Grays) are bad news.

They wipe out the memory of abductees, and totally alter their personality.

They have at their disposal all the mental, intellectual, scientific, paranormal, and physical means and tools to paralyze, handicap, incapacitate, and control the physical, mental, emotional, and psychological faculties of abductees.

Dr. Robert Hutton (Looking at his watch and not listening to Riya-Marjana): Where is everybody? OK, what's your plan now? Are you finally going to deliver your message?

Marjana: Will see. I want to find first, what they have on their mind. I will study their reaction, and I will go from there.
A captain enters the room.
Captain: They are here. Let's go.The Vice President is here too.

Riya-Marjana, Robert and the captain exit the small reception room, take a long and narrow corridor and head toward the meeting room.
The meeting-room. Building "s2".
Time: approximately 11:15/11:20 am.
The room is packed with people. Cameras and electronic sensors everywhere. On the left side of the room, a gigantic map of Europe, Russia, the Middle East, the Near East, Asia, Earth's seas and oceans is pasted on 20 foot long wall. The map looks sterile; it has no luminous dot, slots, and map marking symbols. But its size dominates the room. The three dimensional size of the map seems to hide lots of military secrets. And if you look at the map from a particular angle, it seems to change colors, and particular spots appear to be brighter than the rest of the map.
Present at meeting:
Vice President of the United States
Secretary of Defense
Peggy Arnold, Secretary of Defense's special assistant/aide
Admiral Allan Roscoe
Admiral Roscoe's military aide
Howard Cassey, Director of the CIA
General Ramsey
Director of the Central Intelligence Group
A scientist from Kelley-Koet Manufacturing Company, Kentucky
Brigadier General from NORAD
Brigadier General from Peterson Air Force Base
General Harry McMullen, San Antonio Air Materiel, Kelly Air Force Base, San Antonio, Texas.
General Arnold, USSTRATCOM (United States Strategic Command)
Colonel from Groom Lake Facility
Colonel and a civilian scientist from Ellington Air Force Base (NASA Ellington Field)
Colonel from Groom Lake Test Facility
Colonel from Edwards Air Force Base

Colonel from Hellendale Facility
Military scientist from Brunswick Naval Air Station
Australian scientist from Pine Gap Research Facility
Dr. Robert Hutton
Dr. Jean-Paul Lemaire, Belgian scientist working for NASA
Dr. Benedict Iliescu, American-Romanian cosmologist
Dr. Emanuel Berger
Dr. John Brucker, Army Ballistic Missile Agency Fabrication
Laboratory
Dr. Oswald Gruene, NASA Astrionics Division
Two civilian scientists who worked on "Project Moon Dust", and
"Blue Fly"
Dr. Everest S. Hamilton, MK Ultra Mind Control Program, CIA
Dr. Stanley Bernard, DOE (Department of Energy)
Two high ranking officers, NSA
Two scientists from NRL (United States Naval Research
Laboratory)
Two engineers from Boeing Integrated Defense System
Two engineers from Northrop
A senior scientist from Lockheed
Numerous special agents from various intelligence agencies
Seven unidentified guests
Catholic archbishop of New York
A fleet of cameramen, technicians, photographers,
MPs, military guards, etc.

The captain, Marjana and Dr. Robert Hutton enter the huge meeting room. A major waiting inside, directs Marjana to a low stand situated in front of a large crescent-shaped table where everybody is seated behind. Dr. Robert Hutton takes his seat next to General Ramsey. The Vice President of the United States stands up and with a smile introduces himself to Marjana.

Vice President of the United States: It is a historical moment, and on behalf of the President of the United States and the American people, I welcome you. I am Vice President George Buschwald. Welcome to the United States of America.
Marjana (Smiling and very calmly): I have visited your beautiful country many times before. Thank you for taking the time to see me. I bring you the warm greetings of the Anunnaki Council.

Vice President of the United States (Smiling and very politely): Thank you...Maaada.mmm (Note: He did not know what to call her). Finally he said, madam.

Marjana: Mr. Vice President. I know how you feel being here, looking at a woman from another world.

Vice President of the United States: You bet! How should I call you?

Marjana: Riya Marjana.

Vice President of the United States: Riya. Beautiful. And you are from Ashtari.

Riya-Marjana: You already know who I am.

Vice President of the United States: Not exactly.

Riya-Marjana: You do. I am in what you call the AT; the Aliens Transcripts...The 1947 Meetings with the Ardi-Nishtaar and Zetas?

Vice President of the United States: Yes yes of course.

I remember now. What brings you to America?

Riya-Marjana: You already know Mr. Vice President.

Vice President of the United States: No I don't.

Riya-Marjana: The Protocol?

The TABLET?? 2022?

Vice President of the United States (Looking at Robert Hutton): Oh Yes...Oh yes...General Ramsey and Mr. Cassey told me.... (A long pause) you have a message from your people to our people. And I would like to hear it.

Riya-Marjana: It is more than a message. It is a friendly warning.

Vice President of the United States: Ah? A warning? About what?

Riya-Marjana: I'll get to it later. First let me hear your questions. What do you want to ask me? What do you want to know?

Vice President of the United States: Are you planning on invading Earth?

Riya-Marjana: No. You have nothing to fear.

Vice President of the United States: How about the Dragos?

The Orions? Other civilizations?

Aren't they interested in colonizing Earth?

Riya-Marjana: Advanced civilizations are not interested in you. Even though, Earth is a destination on their passage to other galaxies. Earth is a practical Ba'aab to many civilizations. Their interest ends there. No colonization.

Vice President of the United States: You mean a Stargate?

Riya-Marjana: Yes. The Dragos, The Orions and other civilizations would not survive on your planet. Their body's composition and structure would not allow them to survive for long. The oxygen you breathe is poison to them.

Vice President of the United States: But the Anunnaki...your people would survive?

Riya-Marjana: Of course.

We built your first civilizations in Mesopotamia, Phoenicia, Egypt, Armenia, Turkey, Anatolia. The Anunnaki are among the very few civilizations outside your solar system who look like you.

We created you in our image to a certain degree. But our organism is different.

Vice President of the United States (Looking at Dr. Hutton): I see.

Dr. Jean-Paul Lemaire (Pointing at Riya-Marjana): Mr. Vice President, may I...

Vice President of the United States Interrupting): Sure, go ahead Dr. Lemaire.

Dr. Jean-Paul Lemaire: What can you tell us about the ASC.

The Alien Submerged Crafts?

Riya-Marjana: Ardi-Nishtaar use them to navigate underwater through a web of 17 channels which link them to their habitats, headquarters, bases and communities.

Your scientists coined it the "Net", and "Tubes". They are aquatic cold plasma corridors...undetectable by satellites, sonar or any other underwater detection system.

Dr. Jean-Paul Lemaire (Verbatim and anxious): Bon, how your intergalactic travel is done?

Riya-Marjana: In so many ways. The Ba'aab...the black holes, the white holes. We use dark energy, white energy, dark matter, anti-matter, neutral matter, anti-gravity, and time-space memory.

We bend time, past, present and future...We rewind time. In some dimensions, the future does not exist, in other dimensions, time is another dimension, so we zoom between.

We also travel to universes from the future.

Vice President of the United States (Confused): Could you please explain this?

Riya-Marjana: The universe is one of many multiverses.

It bends on itself and bumps into its multi-layers, constantly creating more universes, including galaxies, and black holes.

Dr. Jean-Paul Lemaire: Indefinitely? And...
Dr. Robert Hutton (Interrupting): Dr. Lemaire, the universe expands in multiple directions, through the "dark energy flow".
If the universe ceases to exist, copies of the extinct universe will re-animate a new beginning which explodes into billions of new universes of all shapes. This how Riya explained it to me, any how.
Dr. Benedict Iliescu: New universes of all shapes. What do you mean Dr. Hutton?
Dr. Robert Hutton: Again, I am quoting Riya; at one point in time, the universe, and the primordial galaxies were flat. And in the dark space of these galaxies, and other time-space-universes were constantly created...flat. That's right. This could happen again, as the universe is constantly expanding.
Dr. Benedict Iliescu (Smiling sarcastically): Flat?
The universe is flat? Ridiculous! We are no longer in the medieval ages, Dr. Hutton.
Dr. Robert Hutton: I didn't say the whole universe is flat, Dr. Iliescu. I said some galaxies were flat at the beginning of the universe...at the beginning of time.
And yes some are still....flat...flat. The flat net of galaxies allows extraterrestrials to bend time and space...This how they create a short cut to other dimensions. Go ahead, ask her yourself.
Dr. Emanuel Berger: (Addressing the question to Riya-Marjana): Is this how your spacecrafts overcome gravity?
Riya-Marjana: Not always. Sometimes is just the opposite.
We take advantage of gravity. Gravity can be used as time-space tunnel. Some universes leak their gravity into other dimensions and galaxies, through the dilatation of Time-Orbits. This gravity has time-space memory. We use time-space memory to get closer to the Time-Orbits which spin our spacecrafts at a speed faster than the speed of light.
Vice President of the United States of America: Is it possible Dr. Lemaire? Dr. Hutton? Faster than the speed of light? Dr. Lemaire?
Dr. Jean Lemaire: I don't know Mr. Vice President. But we already know that our laws of physics are not always the same, everywhere in the universe. So maybe...yes... faster than the speed of light is possible, at least in theory. Albert Einstein's theory has many loopholes. But please don't quote me.
Dr. Emanuel Berger (Asking Riya-Marjana, while looking at Dr. Hutton): What is gravity? And how do you escape gravity?

51

Riya-Marjana: You will never understand what gravity is, as long as you believe time is linear. We escape gravity by zooming into the light of the universe. Light bends on itself. Light curves...one way to shorten distances between stars and galaxies, and escape gravity.

Vice President of the United States: How long it would take your spacecrafts to get to the Moon from any spot on Earth?

Riya-Marjana: A few minutes. In some cases, seconds.

Vice President of the United States: Are you willing to share your technology with us?

Riya-Marjana: I know they are not telling you everything. NASA already knows how...Route Orbital X.

Vice President of the United States: Route Orbital X?

Riya-Marjana: Accessible once every 25 years from Earth, 7 years from Mars, and seconds through the Ba'aab. You tried it twice before and you failed. Next time, try New York and Chicago Ba'aabs. Rewinding time is another possibility. You call it time-travel.

Vice President of the United States (Looking at Admiral Roscoe): Rewinding time. Is it possible?

Vice President of the United States addressing the question to Riya-Marjana: How do you rewind time?

Riya-Marjana: Rewinding time is a child game to us... and to many advanced civilizations. It is not a big deal. Some of you already know what happened in the 1957 meeting with the Ardi-Nishtaar. They told your President...President Eisenhower about time rewinding technology. Your military scientists and your President did not believe it could be done, until the Ardi-Nishtaar rewound the tape of time, and not only projected Jesus Christ in the flesh, but also let everybody hear his voice. Dr von Braush's assistant recorded Jesus Christ's voice on tape. You still have the tape.

General Marshall was present at the meeting, and asked the Ardi-Nishtaar if they could re-project a particular event that occurred in World War II, known only to him, to General Omar Bradley, and to General Patton. He gave the Ardi-Nishtaar the date and location of the event, and waited for the holographic projection. And what they saw, was accurate down to the very last detail.

Secretary of Defense: Hi. I am Albert Wineberger, Secretary of Dense of the United States. I am unaware of that.

Riya-Marjana: Yes I know. You were kept in the dark for so long. Do you know anything about theUnited States Military-Ardi-Nishtaar Vortex Tunnel?

Secretary of Defense: I have no idea and I WANT TO KNOW!

Riya-Marjana: They also kept it secret from you, and from your President. The Vortex Tunnel killed many of your men. It started in the 1965 and became fully operational in 1971. When activated, an invisible vortex opens up, and sucks up everything in its path, up to 500 feet in all directions.

They first used it in the Midwest and killed dozens of farmers in the process, and destroyed many properties. You worked together with the Ardi-Nishtaar.

Vice President of the United States: Are you absolutely sure?

Riya-Marjana: Ask William Colby. (Former CIA Director)

Secretary of Defense: What was the nature...the purpose of Project Vortex Tunnel?

Riya-Marjana: The primary purpose of the project was to propel objects and people into a vacuum tunnel that leads into another dimension. Your military nicknamed it "TTT" or the "Tag Team Tunnel". It is a horrible weapon developed by your allies the Ardi-Nishtaar. It killed 25 soldiers and two scientists. This is the high price you paid for trusting the Ardi-Nishtaar.

Brigadier General from NORAD: Where did they use the Vortex Tunnel? In the Midwest?

Riya-Marjana: I will show you, right now. I am going to project on that wall, actual scenes from the experiments. See for yourself.

Absolute silence in the room. Cameramen get closer, as close as possible to capture the projection on film.

Riya-Marjana holographically projects on the wall, horrible scenes from vortex tunnel experiment.

Scenes: Peoples' heads exploding...farmers agonizing and shredded to pieces in a vacuum tunnel...tornadoes swirling and smashing houses, tractors and bulldozers spinning in the air...and a military crew stationed behind the vacuum tunnel capturing these atrocities on film.

Admiral Allan Roscoe: Mr. Vice President. This is a trick. It never happened.

Riya-Marjana: A trick? So watch this!

Riya-Marjana points her thumb at Admiral Alan Roscoe and lifts him up in mid-air and makes him go up and down, and down and up like a yoyo...He begins to spin, floats right and left, and turns in mid-air, as if he is sucked up by a vacuum cleaner.
Panic spread.
Dr. Robert Hutton: Stop it Riya.

Riya-Marjana drops admiral roscoe on the floor like a sack of potato.
Riya-Marjana: Would you call this a trick too? If I can do it...
The Ardi-Nishtaar can do it too!
Vice President of the United States: I am going to ask for a full investigation. I promise you that! Admiral Roscoe, I expect from you a full report on the Vortex Tunnel.
Admiral Allan Roscoe (Catching his breath and still shaking):
Yes Sir. I didn't know sir. I had no prior knowledge.
Vice President of the United States (Interrupting Roscoe):
Find out Admiral. And I want a full list of the names of the soldiers, the scientists and the people who got killed.
Admiral Allan Roscoe: Yes, Mr.Vice President.
Vice President of the United States: What is going on General Ramsey?
General Ramsey: I don't know sir.It is terrible! It could be one of the CIA black projects? They don't tell us everything, sir.
General Ramsey (Pissed off) whispering in the ear of Admiral Roscoe: Why didn't you tell me about it?
Admiral Allan Roscoe: You don't need to know. You stay out of it.
General Ramsey: Will see about that!
Riya-Marjana: With your permission Mr. Vice President, I would like to visit Dulce Base.
Vice President of the United States: What is so special about Dulce Base?
Riya-Marjana (Smiling): You knew about Dulce Base, long before you became Vice President of the United States.
The Vice President of the United States whispering in the ear of the Secretary of Defense: It's getting dirty. It is very embarrassing. Why should everybody know about this? I am out of here. You are in charge. Deal with it.
The Vice President of the United States excuses himself and leaves the room. Noises in the background. Perfect timing for gossiping.

Attendees start to talk to each other. Almost everybody in the meeting room, suddenly has something to say to the person sitting next to him.

Secretary of Defense (Addressing the attendees): The Vice President has something urgent to attend to. Something came up. Will take a short break, folks.

Absolute silence in the room.

Secretary of Defense (Asking Riya-Marjana): Why do you want to go to Dulce?

Riya-Marjana: Frankly, I do not need your permission.

I can destroy the Base without lifting a finger. You have no idea what I can do. Look at the map.

Riya-Marjana walks toward the map.

She begins to point at several spots on the map. Nobody knows what she is doing!

Riya-Marjana (With a firm voice): Here...here...here...and here...are the secret locations of your nuclear submarines. We know everything about your submarines. In this spot, at a depth of 800 feet, you have a ballistic missile submarine. And here, at a depth of 900 feet, you have an attack submarine. Here, you have your USS Nautilus. And right here, at a depth of 1,000 feet, you have your SSBN 598.

We can destroy your Trident, your Polaris and all your ballistic missiles in seconds. And we can do it from Earth's orbit. You are no match to the Anunnaki!!

Riya-Marjana begins to press with vigor on each spot.

And suddenly each spot catches fire.The whole map is burning. The room is full of heavy black and gray smoke. The awful smell coming from the melting rubber and plastic, from which the map is made of, makes many cough. Many panic, others freeze in their seat...and few take cover. Security guards rush to extinguish the fire. Instantly, the twenty armed soldiers positioned near the front entrance and the back exit of the room take aim at Riya-Marjana. Nine MPs point their automatic assault rifles at Riya-Marjana and move forward.

Theatrical scene at its best, but seriously threatening each person in the room.

Secretary of Defense (Shouting): Hold your fire!

Riya-Marjana: Is this what you want? Do I have your permission to go to Dulce Base?

Secretary of Defense: You made your point. You want to go to Dulce? Go to Dulce. But may I ask why you are so interested in Dulce. And where the hell is Dulce?

Riya-Marjana: I will tell you where Dulce is. It is on the Jicarilla Apache Indian Reservation, under Archuleta Mesa. Dulce is where your government and the Ardi-Nishtaar are conducting genetic experiments on abductees...women...children...where atrocities and crimes are constantly committed by your physicians, and officers collaborators of Ardi-Nishtaar, and where our Tablet is! The Ramadosh Tablet...the space-time calendar.

Secretary of Defense: Is it true, Admiral Roscoe? General Ramsey?

Admiral Roscoe: No sir.....she doesn't know what she is talking about. There is no Dulce Base.

Secretary of Defense: General Ramsey?

General Ramsey: I have no clues, sir. I never heard of Dulce Base before.

Secretary of Defense (Talking to Peggy Arnold, his aide): Peggy, get me the Joint Chief of Staff.

Peggy Arnold phones the Joint Chief of Staff.

Peggy Arnold: He is on the line, sir.

Secretary of Defense General. A quick question.

What do you know about Dulce Base that I don't know?

General Griffith Dulce? Nothing. Why, Mr. Secretary?

Secretary of Defense: Nothing? Absolutely nothing! You don't know what is going on at Dulce, and you never heard of Dulce?

General Griffith: No sir.

Secretary of Defense: Dulce is where the aliens are conducting genetic experiments on abductees, General. So you never heard of Dulce? Or any abduction?

General Griffith: No sir.

Secretary of Defense: I will call you back. Thanks General.

Secretary of Defense: Director Cassey, do you know anything about Dulce?

Director Howard Cassey (Director of the CIA): The Air Force used the base for a few months. But it is abandoned now, Mr. Secretary.

Secretary Defense: There is no Dulce!! Nobody knows a thing about Dulce! The Joint Chief of Staff...General Griffith knows nothing about Dulce...zip! General Ramsey has no clues! The CIA, Director Cassey is telling me, it is an abandoned place. Admiral Roscoe says it does not exist!!

Riya-Marjana: I will take you there Mr. Secretary.
It is an enormous military base with 12 underground levels. As big as The North Side of Area 51. It is a top secret base, your Congress, your President, The White House, The Pentagon, the National Security Advisor, yourself and the American people know nothing about it.
Admiral Allan Roscoe: Mr. Secretary, Mr. Secretary! This woman is lunatic.
Thiiiiiss...Thiiiis woman is not an Anunnaki... Sheee...shheee is just a woman... a shape-shifter from HELL!!! She is the biggest hoax in history!!

Furiously, Dr. Robert Hutton stands up, points his finger at Admiral Roscoe and shouts...
Dr. Robert Hutton: Shut up! Shut up asshole!
Dr. Robert Hutton is transformed into an enraged beast. He is no longer the intellectual man, the quite and down-to-earth historian and polite scholar. He is totally and utterly a different person.
He leaves the table and walks toward Riya-Marjana, stands by her side and holds her hand. Riya-Marjana is delighted. A huge smile on her face. Her face glitters. Everybody could see she is not from hell. With her stunning beauty and grace, she appears to them like an angel from heaven.
Admiral Allan Roscoe (Shouting at Robert): You are a fake! Phony like your bitch! You are finished!
Dr. Robert Hutton: Fuck you!! Fuck you!!
Secretary of Defense: Dr. Hutton, and you Admiral Roscoe... behave, please. Both of you.
Dr. Robert Hutton: Show them Riya...Show them.
Riya-Marjana (Pointing at a curtain on her left): Mr. Secretary, please look at this curtain. Right there, the black velvet curtain, on your right.
Everybody turns his head toward the curtain. The black curtain, hanged from the ceiling like an accordion becomes to flatten gradually. It is totally transformed into a solid white sheet like a huge movie theater's screen.
Admiral Roscoe whispers in the ear of a military man seated next to him (His aide).
Admiral Allan Roscoe: What is she doing now?
Military man: It is too late now, sir.

Dr. Robert Hutton (Talking calmly to the Secretary of Defense): Mr. Secretary, please watch very carefully...And all of you. Riya is going to project on the white screen...right this minute, what the aliens and some of our officers who betrayed our trust and violated the Constitution of the United States of America did at Dulce.
Their horrors and atrocities at Dulce Base!! You are going to see with your own eyes what they did and still doing at Dulce.
On the screen: Dulce Base.
Holographic projection rolling... Scenes of atrocities and genetic manipulations of abductees. Aliens operating on abductees. Dozen of abductees are constantly brought to a large room.
Dr. Robert Hutton: Ladies and gentlemen, what you are looking at, are alien doctors in genetic operations room...they bring in abductees and operate on them.
At the far end, you see military personnel, ours! The walls are highly irregular. Look how they move back and forth, in and out like rubber. On the right, dozens of tables where aliens line up human bodies' parts.
On the left, victims moaning and screaming, they are attached to tubes... watch how the aliens are extracting their blood. In the center under the huge light, watch the needles entering the nose, the mouth and private parts of women.
Right behind them, dozens of sedated children and babies attached to stretchers. Some dead...Some are still alive...and look at those babies who have already lost their eyes. The eyes of the babies were extracted by the aliens. They use them for spare parts. Riya please take over.

Riya-Marjana: Look at the tubes. The Ardi-Nishtaar use them for blood transfusion. The blood of your women and children is sucked up from their bodies and poured into containers. Watch now how human blood is turning blue.
It becomes the Ardi-Nishtaar's blood. Later on, the Ardi-Nishtaar will mix it with cows' blood they mutilated all over America.
Secretary of Defense: Horrifying! Barbaric! Unreal!
General Ramsey: Mother of God!
Dr. Robert Hutton: Next scene. Watch the needles lowered down from the huge machine attached to the ceiling. Watch how they penetrate the bodies of the abductees...their noses, mouths, eyes, under the belly...their genitals.

Abductees are screaming, they faint from pain. On the round tables, under the sensors, watch how the aliens remove babies' eyes from their sockets. It is a massacre, ladies and gentlemen. Look at these men cut in half. They are spare parts.

Are you watching admiral Roscoe???

Women, children, and men who are still alive will be butchered, and their bodies' parts will be stored in jars, containers, tanks, and ice-bags.

Secretary of Defense: What are those things hanging from the rods?

Dr. Robert Hutton: Hooks...Hooks, Mr. Secretary. Hooks for human bodies' parts. Meat hooks like in a slaughter house.

General Ramsey: My God! Mother of God!

Amputated legs, arms...

Dr. Robert Hutton: And hands, lungs, heads!

The nurse standing at the far end of the room faints. Three people vomit. Horrified, cameramen froze. Terror in the room.

Secretary of Defense: I saw enough.

Admiral Allan Roscoe goes ballistic. (Screaming): Mr. Secretary, can't you see? It's a trick? A photo-montage!

(Pointing at Robert, and ordering his men): Arrest him! Arrest this woman!

MPs and 10 soldiers dressed in black rush to arrest Dr. Robert Hutton and Riya-Marjana

Secretary of Defense: Back off! Admiral Roscoe you are relieved of your duty!

Five soldiers are still four feet away from Riyah-Marjana. Instantly Riya-Marjana multiplies herself into 10 different copies; ten Riya-Marjanas in the flesh float in mid-air.

Riya-Marjana (Talking to the soldiers): Which one do you want to arrest?

With piercing eyes she lifts up the men in the air like balloons, and throws them against the wall. Everybody is in a state of shock! Her ten copies dissipate. Riya-Marjana contracts herself and returns to her original shape.

Secretary of Defense (Talking to Riya-Marjana): Go to Dulce...

(Looking at General Ramsey) You too General. I want a full report, pictures, slides, films, get me everything!

Riya-Marjana: Dr. Hutton too. I want him to go with us.

Secretary of Defense: Fine. We have to arrange a transport for you.

Take my plane.
Riya-Marjana: No need Mr. Secretary. Transport is under our feet.
Secretary of Defense: What do you mean?
Dr. Robert Hutton: The tunnels...the tunnels, Mr. Secretary.
There are 25 underground tunnels...Right below us.
Secretary of Defense: Where? Here? At Area 51?
Dr. Robert Hutton: Right here, sir.
They stretch all the way to Washington, DC...The White House,
The Pentagon, the CIA, Langley, Virginia, NASA, Manhattan,
Colorado, Maryland, Florida, Pennsylvania, Alaska, Hawaii, the
Pacific, and Dulce. You name it, sir. They are everywhere!!
Secretary of Defense: I'll be damned!

While Dr. Robert hutton is still talking to the Secretary of Defense,
Admiral Allan Roscoe is whispering in the ear of his military aide,
seated next to him.
Admiral Allan Roscoe: Get rid of them (Referring to Riya-Marjana
and Robert)
Military aide: How?
Admiral Allan Roscoe: Call the Base. Talk to Major Higgins and
Zarro (Note: Zarro is a gigantic alien at Dulce Base). They know
what to do.
The military aide leaves the room from the back door.

Location: Underground of area 51 -UTTCS.
Sergeant Collins takes General Ramsey, Dr. Robert Hutton and
Riya-Marjana to the second level of UTTC (Underground Tram
Transportation Central), also called Central Station, and the
Tram.
A 55 foot high by 45 foot wide compound of underground tunnels
and trains connecting Area 51 to a web of secret undergrounds
facilities and locations around the country.
Trains are coming and going. Lots of activities. Few Grays-aliens
are spotted.
General Ramsey: Where are we, Sergeant?
Sergeant Collins: UTTCS; Central Station, sir
General Ramsey: What what? UT..TC?
Sergeant Collins: They are tracks sir. Track TR1, like Air Force 1,
sir, a direct track to The White House.
General Ramsey: The red one?

Sergeant Collins: TR2P sir, it takes you directly to The Pentagon, And to Washington's National Airport.
General Ramsey: The green one?
Sergeant Collins: We have 2 of those, sir...2 green lines, sir. One to NORAD, one to Canada, sir.
General Ramsey: Canada? How about that! And the gray line?
Sergeant Collins: Straight to Dulce Base, sir.
General Ramsey: Very appropriate.Take me to the gray track. How fast is the train?
Sergeant Collins: Each unit (Car, train) is as fast as OXCART Mach-3, sir.
Dr. Robert Hutton: 3 times faster than the speed of sound.
Riya-Marjana remains quiet. Not a word.
She is observing everything. She can't keep her eyes off Robert.
She reaches for his right hand. Both are smiling. General Ramsey's mind is somewhere else. He mumbles a few words.
Dr. Robert Hutton is laughing.
General Ramsey: What are you laughing at?
Dr. Robert Hutton: A sergeant knows more than a 2 star General.
General Ramsey (Highly upset): Tell me about it!! Gray line, green line, red line...tracks tracks...Canada... Roscoe son of a bitch!

Location: Inside the train.
Sergeant Collins, General Ramsey, Dr. Robert Hutton and Riya-Marjana enter the gray train. Sergeant Collins gives instruction to General Ramsey on how to operate the train.
Sergeant Collins: It is easy sir to operate the unit. You push the gray button, here sir, and you are on your way to Dulce, sir. You will be there in a few minutes.
General Ramsey: The black one?
Sergeant Collins: This will bring you back, sir.
General Ramsey: And the red one?
Sergeant Collins: If you want to stop, sir.
General Ramsey (Pointing at a square on a small dashboard): What's this?
Sergeant Collins: Emergency sir. But nobody uses it, sir. Security will know immediately if something is wrong, sir.

Location: At the Dulce base —second level's entrance.

They exit the train and reach Dulce Base's second underground level. Two men in black uniforms and a Major standing by the gate open an immense metallic door leading to the main hall.

General Ramsey: I am General Ramsey.
Major (Saluting): Major Glennan, sir. We were expecting you.
General Ramsey: Who is in charge here? Who is you commanding officer?
Major: Admiral Allan Roscoe, sir.
General Ramsey: Who???? Roscoe!! Roscoe again! The son of a bitch! I never trusted this bastard.
Riya-Marjana: Surprised, General?
General Ramsey: You bet your ass lady. Pardon me Madam. I should have known. Roscoe, the fuckin' piece of shit!! Sorry again my lady. Excuse my French.
Dr. Robert Hutton: Expect more surprises, General.
General Ramsey: Major, let's start with the first floor.
Major: Sir, the first floor is closed. We sealed the area...We had major radio-active le....
General Ramsey (Interrupting): Never mind, Major. Take me to the second floor, then.
Major: We are on the second floor, sir.

Dulce Base-second level.
Starting from the second level, compartments are divided into large operation rooms, separated by elaborate long corridors, curving at 90 degrees every hundred feet or so, with doors dropping down from the ceiling to seal off segments of the compound, in the event of radiation leakage, or any matter related to internal security. Doors in the corridors have circular porthole-like windows within what is a whitish metal of extraterrestrial origin.
None of these metallic alloys are made on Earth, due to Earth's gravity, and as such have to be done in orbit aboard an alien ship.
The Major takes them through a long corridor leading to a dark small room.
They enter the room, and get into some sort of a square vehicle with a silvery metallic spinning top, approximately 8ft in diameter. It corkscrews its way downwards centrifugally around a rod using a form of magnetic propulsion.

General Ramsey (Asking the Major): What do you call this...this vehicle?
Major: SMS. "Spinning Mobile Satellite"
General Ramsey: Very fancy.
What the hell is Spinning Mobile Satellite? Forget it.

The vehicle stops. They exit the SMS.
Major Glennan: This way, sir.
General Ramsey: Where to? Where are we now, Major?
Major Glennan: We are almost there, sir.
We have to take the elevator down to the first compartment of the second floor.
Inside the elevator:
They get into a fiberglass box (elevator). General Ramsey notices the elevator has no cables.
General Ramsey: No cables? Where are the cables of the elevator?
Major Glennan: It operates electronically...magnetically, sir.
General Ramsey: Alien technology!
Major Glennan: Yes sir. We don't have electrical wirings on the Base. Everything is controlled electronically.
General Ramsey nodding his head.
General Ramsey: No MPs I don't see any security guards here?
No Guards
Major Glennan: Security is very tight on the Base, sir.
General Ramsey: Security face recognition, voice recognition.
Major Glennan: No sir. We use the latest alien technology on the Base.
Riya-Marjana: Breath recognition, General.
They check your breath. You exhale on a screen, and the screen identifies who you are.

Location: The Blue Board Small Room/Compartment 1-level 2:
Finally, they reach compartment 1-level 2. They step inside an oval room. A huge blue-gray board pasted on a wall displays names, numbers, symbols and pushpins in various colors. Each pushpin emits different light's sparkle.
General Ramsey: That's it? One room?
Major Glennan: No sir. You have to push on this (Pushpin), and you will see...

General Ramsey (Interrupting): See what?

Major Glennan: If you touch the gray pin, one of the hidden doors in the room will open up, you walk on a magnetic pad and it will take you straight to the aliens' headquarters. If you touch the red pin, you will be directed to the hospital. If you touch the silver pin, another door opens up, you ride a trolley, and it will take you to the anti-gravity flying discs, you might call it UFOs if you want. So on.

General Ramsey: Take me to the hospital?

Location: Genetic operations ward.

Major Glennan touches the red pin. A door opens up. They all step on a magnetic pad. The pad slides its way to a huge ward, where dozens of aliens are seen operating on patients.

Hundreds of surgical tables lined up one after another in double rows, separate the alien doctors from an area designated to impregnate women abducted from all over the United States.

They keep walking and reach an area designated for removal of fetuses.

Four aliens and one civilian doctor are seen placing fetuses in incubators which create hybrids.

Then they turn right and enter another room packed with cribs, and some sort of gluey blue-liquid tanks full of human bodies' parts; hands, feet, legs, bones, heads, eyes, amputated arms, livers, hearts, lungs, penises.

At the very end of the room under a series or arches, they find horrifying-looking bestial creatures inside hexagonal and spherical cages, moaning, shouting and screaming like mad dogs. Some looked reptilians with three eyes, others like apes, and a few, like medieval gargoyles.

On the left side of the ward, a huge corridor leads them to a round room packed with aliens, harvesting human tissues.

Two long and narrow shelves, containing a large quantity of animals' part, (mostly cows) could not be missed.

General Ramsey: I saw enough. Major, tell me something…
Does the Joint Chief of Staff ever visit the Base?

Major Glennan: He was here the last week, sir.

General Ramsey: The Vice President?

Major Glennan: Who sir?

General Ramsey: The Vice President of the United States?
Major Glennan: No sir. I don't know, sir. I don't think so, sir.
General Ramsey: Let's get out of here...

Alihiyat: Ulemite/Arabic. Noun.
It is the study of the nature of God and origin of religions. An in-depth socio-historical analysis of the origin of mankind, the implication of terrestrial religious beliefs, and how new religious dogmas, concepts and stories are usually taken from anterior religious scriptures written hundreds, probably thousands of years earlier. Alihiyat derived from the Ana'kh word "A-li-iyat".
And from Alihiyat, the pre-Islamic words Ali, Ilahi, and Ilah, came to life, and which mean God.
(The God as understood and worshipped according to the Judeo-Christian-Muslim tradition.)
A minor part of the Ailihiyat focuses on the origin of the Hebraic religion, and the influence of other civilizations and religions (Such as Phoenician, Ugaritic, Egyptian) on the Jewish religion, and the writing of the Bible.
This study was popular among Ulema's students during the 3rd century B.C. Basically, it echoes what authors and free-spirited theologians of the 19th, and 20th centuries thought about the origin and nature of Yahweh, Jehovah, God, Allah.

Alkabetz, Shlomo Halevi (1500-1580): Hebrew. Noun.
A Kabbalist, poet, and a secret Anunnaki-Ulema, best known for his song Lecha Dodi. At age 29, he married the daughter of the wealthy Yizchak Cohen of Salonika, but settled in Adrianople, Turkey, where he wrote many of his books, including Beit Hashem, Avotot Ahava, Ayelet Ahavim and Brit HaLevi.
He associated with a group of well-known Kabbalists. Many of his students achieved fame, and his brother in law was the famous Moshe Cordovero (Ramak).
One evening, during the recitation of certain texts, the entire group had a joint vision, where the Shekhinah joined them and told them that they should be moving to the Land of Israel. Apparently she spoke out of the mouth of one of the assembly, but it was not his voice, rather, it was a very pleasant but strong voice that they did not recognize.

Alkabetz, along with some of the others, obeyed the Shekhinah and moved to the Land of Israel, where they settled in Safed, a town well known for its group of Kabbalists. From the book "Anunnaki and Ulema Who's Who", co-authored by Maximillien de Lafayette and Dr. Anbel.

All-Sky Survey, "Cosmic Lens All-Sky Survey/CLASS":
Name for an international scientific collaboration project, created to map radio sources, and study radio gravitational lensed systems. The project was initiated by the United States, Holland, and the United Kingdom.
It was reported but never confirmed that CLASS has intercepted an extraterrestrial communication between two alien spaceships. A SETI's insider claimed that the "WOW Signal", detected on the night of August 15, 1977 at the Ohio Stat University Big Ear Observatory, was indeed a communication between two extraterrestrial spaceships.

Alla Xul: Anunnaki/Ulemite/Sumerian. Noun. Name of one of the Anunnaki's "Fallen Angels", who became an evil god in the Sumerian pantheon.

ALLO/NSA: A division of the National Security Agency in charge of decoding messages, monitoring international communications, and gathering information about UFOs, UFOs' sightings, UFOs' crashes, and alien spaceships. It is also known as the "G Group".

Alma: Acronym for Atacama Large Millimeter/submillimeter Array.
Alma's statement: "The Atacama Large Millimeter/submillimeter Array (ALMA) is a revolutionary instrument in its scientific concept, its engineering design, and its organization as a global scientific endeavor. Currently under construction in the thin, dry air of northern Chile's Atacama Desert at an altitude of 5,000 meters above sea level, ALMA will initially be composed of 66 high-precision antennas working together at millimeter and submillimeter wavelengths, with a possible extension in the future. Thanks to its high resolution and sensitivity, ALMA will open an entirely new "window" on the Universe, allowing scientists to unravel longstanding and important astronomical mysteries, in search of our Cosmic Origins.

ALMA

Some people say that the sun never sets on ALMA. Indeed, ALMA is a wonderful example of a worldwide collaboration, involving partners from four continents. By working together, scientists and engineers from around the world tackle unprecedented challenges and will seek to expand the frontiers of knowledge.

ALMA is expected to begin science operations with a limited number of antennas and to start full science operations with 66 antennas. Scientists from around the world will thus soon employ this remarkable facility to probe the very first stars and galaxies, and directly image exo-planets, possibly discovering the first traces of life."

Alpha Centauri's Akon: Akon is the name of an extraterrestrial being from Apha Centauri who married Elizabeth Klarer, and their union produced a child who currently lives on his planet Meton with his alien father, as claimed by Klarer, who wrote a fabulous book on the subject, titled "Beyond the Light Barrier". The book is highly recommended. A brief description of the book provided by the publisher: This is the autobiographical story of Elizabeth Klarer, a South African woman, and Akon, an astrophysicist from

Meton, a planet of Proxima Centuri that, at a distance of about 4.3 light years, is our nearest stellar neighbor.

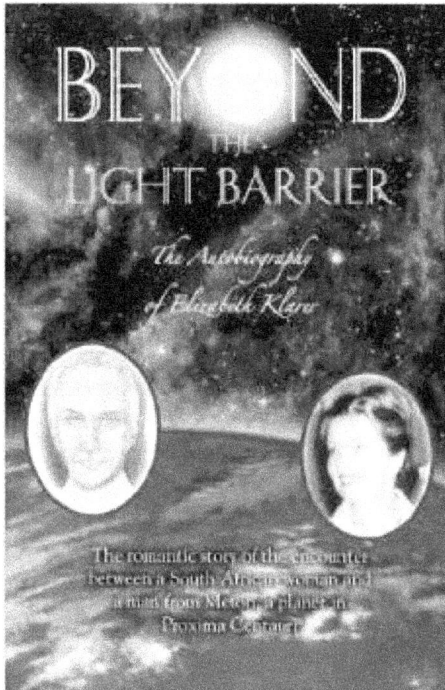

Cover of the book "Beyond the Light Barrier" by Elizabeth Klarer. A masterpiece in the genre.

Elizabeth was taken in his spaceship to Meton, where she lived with him and his family for four months and where she bore his child. Her life on Meton is fascinatingly described. Akon brought Elizabeth back to Earth after the birth of their son and continued to visit her thereafter. Akon explained how his spaceship's light-propulsion technology operated, and how it allowed him and his people to travel across vast interstellar distances.

This technology is explained in detail in the book. Elizabeth was given a standing ovation at the 11th International Congress of UFO Research Groups at Weisbaden in 1975, and her speech as guest of honor was applauded by scientists of twenty-two nations.

Elizabeth Klarer (1910-1944).

Elizabeth Klarer with the bust of her alien husband Akon from Meton, a planet of Proxima Centuri.

Alpha Recovery Team (ART): A military unit established by the Pentagon, for the sole purpose of retrieving crashed UFOs, and gathering evidential data on UFOs' sightings in the United States. It is headquartered at Wright Patterson Air Force Base.

Alshich, Moshe (1508-1593): Hebrew. Noun.
A Kabbalist and a secret Anunnaki-Ulema, Moshe Alshich was born in Turkey and lived in Safed, in the Land of Israel. He was a student of Joseph Karo, and was known as Hakadosh – the holy one – a title that few rabbis have attained in Jewish history.
He had some students who had achieved greatness as well, including Rabbi Hayim Vital.
As is the case with many rabbis who were Anunnaki-Ulema as well, very little is known about his private life. He was well known for his commentaries, which are still highly respected. From the book "Anunnaki and Ulema Who's Who", co-authored by Maximillien de Lafayette and Dr. Anbel.

Altercations incidents between the Grays, the military, and scientists:
These altercations refer to the famous "Dulce War" between extraterrestrials and US military; several altercation incidents between the United States military/civilian workers and the aliens, particularly the Greys and the Orions.
In the Aliens Transcripts, a reference was made to altercation incidents between the military, civilian workers (Scientists, contractors, men and women) and the aliens, at underground secret bases.
A significant altercation occurred between the military and the aliens at Dulce Base laboratory. A special armed forces unit was called in to free a number of military personnel and scientists "trapped in the facility who had become aware of what was really going on." 66 soldiers were killed in the effort, and the scientists were not freed. Apparently, an agreement has been reached between the military and aliens who co-shared a secret military base, giving the aliens absolute freedom in conducting their own business in the base.
The soldiers and scientists were restricted from interfering in any activity and genetic operations conducted by the alien Grays.

In addition, it was agreed upon by both parties, that the soldiers shall not bear arms in the areas under the direct control of the aliens. For some reasons, source said, "armed men entered two aliens' compartments carrying sophisticated weapons and laser-beam guns. A clash between the aliens and the military men led to several fatalities. None of the alien Greys was killed."

One report said that "Security guards who worked at Dulce Base were regularly transferred to other units, their names and serial numbers altered, so to hide all evidences and to prevent any possible leak.

By 1983, the military learned about the aliens' agenda, and the full scale of their extensive abduction operations all over the country. Following the clash, members of the Committee... (Name could not be revealed) met at a country club to discuss the whole story and how to deal with the aliens.

The Country Club is a remote lodge with a private golf course, comfortable sleeping and working quarters and its own private airstrip. Some members of the Committee who were in the military, wanted to confess the whole scheme and go public, beg for forgiveness and ask for public support.

Other members of the Committee argued that there was no way they could do that - that the situation was untenable and there was no need in exciting the public with the "horrible truth", and that the best plan was to continue the development of a weapon or plan of containment that could be used against the aliens under the guise of "SDI", the so-called Strategic Defense Initiative which had nothing whatsoever to do with a defense for inbound Russian nuclear missiles.

Alu: Name of the first created man-form with mental faculties. See Abel.

Alubatasharim: Anunnaki/Ulemite. Noun.
A sort of a laser-beam instrument used by the Anunnaki's second expedition during their underwater mining in the Mediterranean Sea. Contray to a popular belief, the Anunnaki did not land on Earth to mine gold, but to mine the red and blue algae in the Mediterranean sea, on the shore of Phoenicia.

71

The Anunnaki had plenty of gold on their planet (Ashtari), and neighboring stars. Anunnaki-Ulema Oppenheimer said, "With their highly advanced technology, transmuting metals into gold, is a child game for the Anunnaki."

Alusharshid: Akkadian. Noun. He was the king of Kish, and the conqueror of Elam. An Anunnaki king who ruled for 36,000 years.

Amalantrah Working: In March 1918, Aleister Crowley has claimed that he succeeded in creating a vortex-gate that links our physical world to a non-physical world.

Aleister Crowley

72

He called it the bridge, and the process was coined the Amalantrah Working. Crowley stated that while the gate (Vortex) was open, an entity manifested itself. Crowley named the entity "Lam".
Later on, he drew a facial portrait of Lam. And lam became a permanent fixture on the landscape of modern ufology. Numerous new age ufology enthusiasts rushed to describe Lam as a Gray!

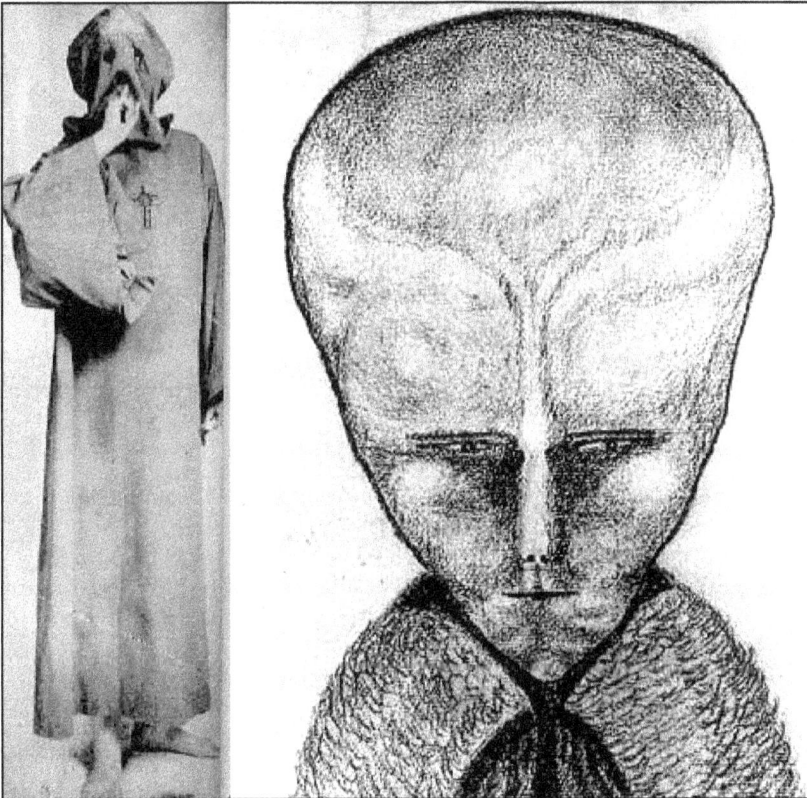

Aleister Crowley and Lam.

Jack Parsons

Some thirty years later, the legendary scientist Jack Parsons and L. Ron Hubbard, founder of Church of Scientology began to work on their "Babalon Working" in a desperate attempt to reopen the gate, allegedly created by Aleister Crowley.

Their fans are convinced that Parsons and Hubbard succeeded in opening the gate, and in allowing entities from a different world to enter and exit the gateway. Some have claimed that an open gate would allow extraterrestrial beings, and particularly the Grays to abduct humans. Nonsense!

L. Ron Hubbard, founder of Church of Scientology.

AMC: Acronym for the United States Air Material Command, Wright Field, later called Wright Patterson Air Force Base.
Ufologists believe that the base is where the Roswell's UFO crash debris were taken to, and stored in one of its secret underground hangars, Hangar 18, more presisely.

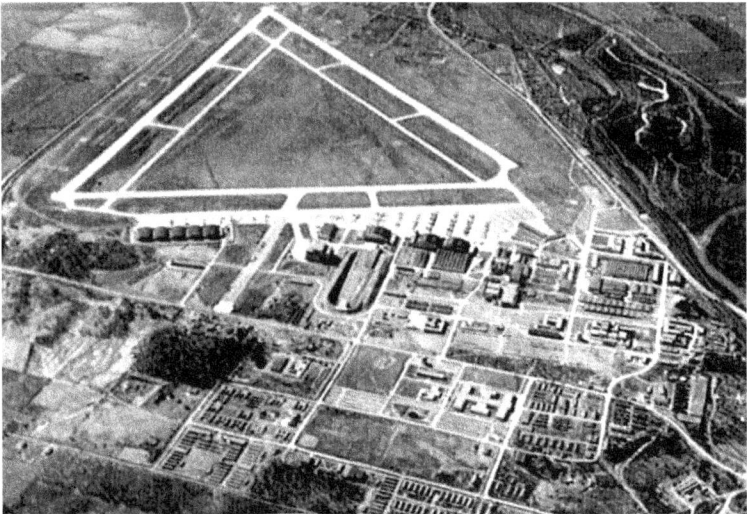
Wright Field.

Lt. Colonel Philip J. Corso claimed that he opened one of the boxes (trunks) which were transported to Wright Patterson and saw an alien body, three to four 4 foot tall, preserved in blue liquid.
See: Corso, Lt. Colonel Philip.

Lt. Colonel Philip J. Corso.

Amelon: Anunnaki/Akkadian. Noun.
Name of an Anunnaki-Akkadian hero who ruled for 46,800 years.

American Association for the Advancement of Science (AAAS): In 1969, AAAS in its annual meeting, included a session on UFOs, despite bitter objection from its members and Donald Menzel. In that historic session, Dr. James McDonald presented a symposium on UFOs. This event was unprecedented in the history of the association.
Another distinguished presenter of UFOs' cases was Dr. J. Allen Hynek, a former chairperson of the Department of Astronomy at Northwestern University, and scientific consultant to Project Blue Book. Both scientists became strong believers in UFOs and alien phenomena.
See: McDonald, Dr. James. Hynek, Dr. J. Allen.

American Ba'ab: A most unusual claim about the American Ba'ab stated that in 2006, while an American spaceship tried to enter a Ba'ab, a GG (Acronym for a "giant Gray") exited the spacecraft, because it needed a sudden repair.
The alien was sucked up into the galactic vacuum and the craft exploded. This event was recorded on a film and was sent to NASA and MIT.

American Institute of Astronautics and Aeronautics (AIAA): The Institute took a daring initiative to bring the attention of American scientists to the UFO phenomenon. In fact,

in 1970, the Institute established a subcommittee to "gain a fresh and unbiased perspective on the UFO question."
A distinguished scientist, Pete A Surrock played a major role in that initiative.

American Presidents & UFOs: President Reagan reported seeing UFOs!

Photo: Lucille Ball.

77

Lucille Ball: "Well...he (President Reagan) told me he saw a UFO...Nancy was there. Why don't you ask Steve Allen?"
Steve Allen and Lucille Ball told us that President Ronald Reagan said to them that he (And Nancy) saw UFOs on two occasions; the first one occurred in 1953, and the second one in 1974.

President Reagan once said in public: "I was in a plane last week when I looked out the window and saw this white light. It was zigzagging around. I went up to the pilot and said, 'Have you seen anything like that before?' He was shocked and said, 'Nope.' And I said to him: 'Let's follow it!'
We followed it for several minutes. It was a bright greenish-white light. We followed it to Bakersfield, and all of a sudden to our utter amazement it went straight up into the heavens. When we got off the plane, I told Nancy all about it."

*** *** ***

President Reagan discussing UFOs and aliens' threats with Shevardnadze and Gorbachev.

September 15, 1987: While having a lunch with Shevardnadze, President Reagan talked with his guest about a possible threat to Earth from out of this world, and asked him, "Do you think the United States and the Soviet Union would be together to fight the threat?" and with a firm tone Mr. Shevardnadze replied, "Absolutely!"
A White House transcript referred to what President Reagan said to Gorbachev about UFOs and aliens; here is an excerpt: "How easy his (Gorbachev) task and mine might be in these meetings that we held if suddenly there was a threat to this world from some other species from another planet outside in the universe. We'd forget all the little local differences that we have between our countries ..."
In 1987, in Moscow, Gorbachev stated that such discussion did occur. Here is an excerpt from Gorbachev's statement, "The U.S. President said that if the earth faced an invasion by extraterrestrials, the United States and the Soviet Union would join forces to repel such an invasion.
I shall not dispute the hypothesis..."

President Ronald Reagan speaking about an alien threat at the United Nations.

Excerpts from President Reagan's Address to the 42nd Session of the United Nations General Assembly in New York, at 11:02 A.M. in the General Assembly Hall, on September 21, 1987.

Ronald Reagan: "We look forward to a time when things we now regard as sources of friction and even danger can become examples of cooperation between ourselves and the Soviet Union. Can we and all nations not live in peace?

In our obsession with antagonisms of the moment, we often forget how much unites all the members of humanity. Perhaps we need some outside, universal threat to make us recognize this common bond. I occasionally think how quickly our differences worldwide would vanish if we were facing an alien threat from outside this world.

And yet, I ask you, is not an alien force already among us? What could be more alien to the universal aspirations of our peoples than war and the threat of war?"

In brief secret meetings, President Reagan echoed his concerns about UFOs' threats to Prime Minister Mohammed Khan Junejo of Pakistan, and UN Secretary General Javier Perez de Cuellar de la Guerra.

Admiral Crowe discussing UFOs with President Reagan and Prime Minister Margaret Thatcher.

Admiral William James Crowe, Jr., Chairman of the Joint Chiefs of Staff, talking to President Reagan: "German UFOs are no threat to national security."

President Reagan also discussed the UFOs' threat with Admiral William James Crowe, Jr., Chairman of the Joint Chiefs of Staff. Both men knew that UFOs were not of an alien origin, but rather a mind-blowing German technology.

President Reagan had limited access to the government's secret files on German UFOs. Admiral Crowe reassured the President that the German UFOs are no threat to national security. He added that President Truman and President Eisenhower had some sort of an agreement with the "old school" and remnants of Nazi scientists who previously worked on these UFOs in Germany, Austria and Poland, and who are currently operating from Canada, Argentina and the Antarctic.

While serving as the U.S. ambassador to Great Britain (1994-97), the Admiral had intensive talks with Prime Minister Margaret Thatcher about the Falklands war, and of course the UFOs. And again, he reassured the Prime Minister that the German UFOs are no threat to Great Britain and the United States.

Jackie Gleason UFO Shocker!

I SAW BODIES OF DEAD ALIENS AT TOP-SECRET AIR FORCE BASE

If Jackie said so, it must be true: Gleason spills the beans on the Feds.

President Nixon saw UFOs and much more!!
The account of Jackie Gleason.

Insiders as well as Jackie Gleason's own accounts revealed that "The Great One", thanks to President Richard Nixon (The Darling of the CIA) had access to secret German UFOs' files, reports on extraterrestrials, and more significantly, secret storage rooms at Homestead Air Force, where he saw with own eyes dead alien bodies. It did not take Gleason long to represent what he saw, for short after, he built a house to resemble a German UFO he saw, and called it "The Mothership".

Sheila MacRae: "Jackie told me the UFOs are real. The Air force got them...some were aliens...some were Germans..."
Sheila MacRae (Alice Kramden) from the "Honeymooners", said Jackie described to her in detail the exterior and interior of UFOs and how concerned was the Air Force. He also told MacRae that these UFOs were made in Germany during the Second World War and the huge ones were made by German scientists who escaped Germany at the end of the war.

Jackie Gleason storage house in Peekskill, New York.
Gleason built a house in Peekskill, N.Y. which he called "The Mothership" at Rock Hill Drive, Cortlandt Manor, NY, north of the intersection of Washington Street and Furnace Dock Road, to remind him of the German UFO he saw.

Photo: Sheila MacRae.
Bob Considine said that Gleason told the truth and President Richard Nixon was very-well informed about the German UFOs, not only that, but four of our Presidents were briefed on Germany's UFOs by the United States Air Force, and all covered-up the whole thing.

Photo: Beverly McKittrick Gleason with husband Jackie Gleason.

Beverly Gleason, (Jackie Gleason's second wife) told friends, movie stars and the media that her husband in the company of President Richard Nixon, saw the bodies of dead aliens in South Florida in 1973 or 1974.

She said verbatim, "After he got back, he was very pleased he had an opportunity to see the dead little men in cases."

When the word got out, Jackie Gleason did not deny the story.

In fact, in 1987, Jackie Gleason told Larry Warren, who was stationed at RAF Bentwaters in Great Britain where he served in the Air Force Security Police of the base.

Mrs. Gleason added that President Richard Nixon took her husband to Homestead Air Force Base where he saw with his own eyes small aliens in a secret storage area. Jackie Gleason confirmed the story on several occasions, and gave additional stunning details.

He stated that he went (with President Nixon) through few areas and laboratories at the Base, until both of them reached a room, where and when President Nixon told him that this very room was the storage room of the wreckage of a flying saucer and the remains of dead aliens' bodies placed in large wooden containers. Then, the President and Gleason entered another larger room, and saw six or eight glass-topped containers/freezers containing the remains of some mangled creatures which did not look humans at all.

Beverly McKittrick, Gleason: "Richard Nixon told Jackie that the UFOs were made by the Germans."

Beverly was really confused because her husband kept changing particular segments from his story. Sometime he would tell his wife that the dead bodies the Army retrieved were aliens, and when he was not drinking too much, he would say the UFOs were German-made, but some of the UFOs were piloted by aliens.

Lucille Ball said that Jackie Gleason did tell her a lot about German UFOs but she did not take him seriously.

According to Lucille, Gleason said that Richard Nixon told him that all the former Presidents knew very well what was going on, and that the Germans were flying their UFOs over the United States as a "Challenge".

Gleason stated that the President of the United States knew that the UFOs were real, and a few years later, after the collapse of Nazi Germany, we (U.S.) collaborated with UFOs' German scientists brought to America from Germany, Austria and Poland.

General R. O'Donnell: "Jackie's right."

Photo: General Emmett "Rosie" O'Donnell.

General R. O'Donnell, then, head of the Strategic Air Force Command, who was listening to Jackie Gleason while talking to columnist Bob Considine, smiled and said verbatim: "Jackie's right."

*** *** ***

84

Jackie Gleason Saw Bodies of Space Aliens at Air Force Base

By BEVERLY GLEASON

Space aliens exist! Ask Jackie Gleason — he's actually seen them.

I'll never forget the night in 1973 my famous husband came home, slumped white-faced in an armchair and spilled out the incredible story to me.

He was late. It was around 11:30 p.m. and I'd been worried. As soon as I heard his key turn in the lock of our golf course home in Inverrary, Fla., I jumped to my feet and asked, "Where have you been?"

His reply stunned me:

"I've been at Homestead Air Force Base — and

President Nixon Arranged for Him To See Them

I've seen the bodies of some aliens from outer space.

"It's top secret. Only a few people know. But the President arranged for me to be escorted in there and see them."

I knew that he and President Nixon were buddies, so it didn't surprise me. But the story that followed was incredible.

"No one would tell me the full details, but a spacecraft is obviously crashed near here," said Jack.

"When I arrived at the base, I was given a heavily armed military escort and driven to a building in a remote area.

"We had to pass a guard at the door, then were shown into a large room.

"And there were the aliens, lying on four separate tables.

belief in the occult and in UFOs.

He read anything he could get his hands on about new UFO sightings around the world.

"You see — there's another one," he'd say, pointing to an article about a sighting.

He was fiercely patriotic and even paid his taxes happily.

But one thing he detested about the government was what he called its cover-up on UFOs.

"They know all about

A FIRM BELIEVER in UFOs, Jackie Gleason actually saw the bodies of space aliens, according to his ex-wife Beverly, shown at left with Gleason as they posed happily on their wedding day.

municate with them," he'd insist.

And he was triumphant when his own beliefs were bolstered by a backstage meeting with one of the astronauts.

Jack was co-hosting a TV show, and one of the guests this night was one of the early American adventurers in space.

When the show was over, Jack and the astronaut became absorbed in a private discussion about UFOs. And when Jack told the man that he was a believer in UFOs, the astronaut confided to him:

"You're right. They do

coming from a friendly place, and we should communicate

"They were tiny — only about two feet tall — with small bald heads and disproportionately large ears.

"They must have been dead for some time because they'd been embalmed."

I started to smile. It seemed just too much to believe.

But Jack caught my look and stared at me for a long time, his face haggard.

"It sounds incredible, but I swear it's true," he said. "I'll never forget it ... ever."

exist. I've seen one with my own eyes during our mission.

"But we've been sworn to secrecy, and the government will never let the information out to the public."

Jack was thrilled — and furious. He was thrilled to be proved right at last, furious to have his theories about a cover-up confirmed.

And, of course, actually seeing the bodies of those aliens was the final proof.

He's intrigued by anything involving the psychic and the occult. He has thousands of books in his library and many of them deal with supernatural subjects.

There was no doubt in Jack's mind that he had lived before, as a swashbuckling English duke in the days of King Henry VIII.

His life as a 16th-century duke had evidently been just as exciting as his present one. He'd tell me how in his nighttime dreams he rode into battle, dressed in a suit of gleaming armor and mounted on a snow white horse. Of course, he was always victorious!

And through his dreams he would recall how he lived

The story of Jackie Gleason, President Nixon and the aliens' bodies written by Beverly Gleason and published in the "National Enquirer" on 8, 17, 1983.

85

President George Bush Sr.
Some passages taken from official reports but never mentioned in the AT (Aliens Transcripts,) clearly indicated that President George Bush Sr., is one of the most knowledgeable persons on the subjects of extraterrestrials, alien abduction, alien technology, and their spacecrafts. President Bush had a direct access to the Aliens Transcripts, Top Secret and Above Top Secret reports, studies and testimonies from civilians and the military (Army senior officers, air force commanders and pilots), and other semi-official and governmental agencies.
While serving as Director of the Central Intelligence Agency (CIA), President Bush gathered and reviewed the world most detailed and documented reports and findings on aliens' spacecrafts, their technology, and extraterrestrials, including their interactions with a few "non-human beings."
President George Bush's files on UFOs and extraterrestrials are nowhere to be found. But they DID exist!
We see all our presidents (Past and present) smiling when reporters ask them questions about UFOs. Some, like President Truman and President Bill Clinton would smile and answer in a humorous manner, others like President George Bush Sr. and President George Bush Jr. would evade the questions, etc.
But now, everything has changed, and the humor and the smiles would no longer do the trick, for the German New World Order's UFOs has become a serious threat.
You should know that it was never the intention of the CIA as an entity to mislead the general public on matters and issues related to alien technology, the UFO phenomena, and other pertinent subjects. Misleading was NOT the CIA objective. Look for your answers in the Oval Office and secret files of the USAF, and nowadays in the drawers of NASA. The CIA and the NSA quite rightfully and legally withheld delicate information on these subjects because revealing such information and declassifying certain files will absolutely jeopardize national security, the safety and sanity of the American people, as well as many people around the globe. It was not the CIA or the NSA which decided to keep the UFO question an Above Top Secret matter, but two powerful (Former) Presidents, and an extremely influential committee/panel consisting of Archbishops, some of the nations' leading businessmen, and of course extremely influential generals and admirals from the army, the navy and the air force.

United States presidents and senators are not allowed to view UFOs' secret files!

When he assumed the office of the President of the United States, President Jimmy Carter summoned George Bush, Sr., then, Director of the CIA, and asked him to be provided with the CIA's files on UFOs.

The Director replied that those files are classified "Above Top Secret" and he (The President) does not have enough "Security Clearance" to see the files, because they were classified under the jargon "No Need To Know".

In other words, President Carter was not allowed to view the UFOs CIA files, because he "did-not-need-to know!"

-Go figure!!

President Carter was shocked!

Then he asked the Director, what he had to do to see those file, and the Director candidly but firmly told him that he must ask a certain congressional committee to declassify those file.

The President was furious, and at one time he tried to get rid of the CIA, but of course he failed.

President Richard Nixon was the only American President who had access to the UFOs' secret files.

Senators too are not permitted to view UFOs' files or even to ask to view them!

When Senator Barry Goldwater tried to view some UFOs' files, and see the Blue Room, at Wright-Patterson Air Force Base, where allegedly 3 aliens' dead bodies were stored, the Senator was refused entry. On more than one occasion, the Senator told the story of being denied access to view the secret underground facilities at the base.

Senator Barry M. Goldwater's statement on the Larry King Show.

In 1994, in an interview conducted by Larry King and broadcast on CNN, Goldwater said, "I think at Wright-Patterson, if you could get into certain places, you'd find out what the Air Force and the government does know about UFOs.

Reportedly, a spaceship landed. It was all hushed up. I called Curtis LeMay and I said, 'General, I know we have a room at Wright-Patterson where you put all this secret stuff. Could I go in there?'

87

I've never heard General LeMay get mad, but he got madder than hell at me, cussed me out, and said, "Don't ever ask me that question again!"

Senator Barry M. Goldwater, a powerful politician, a former presidential candidate, a former Major General in the United States Army Air Corp, and a member of the US Senate Select Committee on Intelligence for many years, could not see the UFOs' files and enter the "Blue Room".
Senator Goldwater continues, "I have investigated that incident (Roswell) through every possible agency that may have had some responsibility, the FBI (Hoover who shut me off quickly), The NRO, DIA, NSA, etc., and have gained nothing other than hell from the Pentagon. I'm as curious about those facts as you.

The reaction I have had from General LeMay and the on-site Roswell facts known by General "Butch" Blanchard, etc., has told me one thing that it did happen and is a major secret regarding UFOs and aliens of our time. Perhaps of all time.
General LeMay Chairman of the Military Joint Chiefs of Staff at the Pentagon very angrily told me that I had no need to know. Butch Blanchard was a very valued friend of mine since WWII. He was the person who announced that a disc had crashed near Roswell in 1947.

This cussing out did awaken me to one fact, that the UFO situation is the highest level of national secrecy... Much higher than the H-Bomb was and more than anything else that is known within the Pentagon, FBI, CIA, DIA, NSA, etc.
That is, nothing is higher security than aliens being here on this planet. Then I realized Curtis was correct. And I never again approached him on the subject. That seemed to prove to me that UFOs were a fact, and do exist.
But, are they all aliens?
I highly suspect a majority are!
Hell, they are no doubt far ahead of our level of intelligence."

*** *** ***

88

Senator Goldwater was denied access to the government's secret files
on UFOs.

General LeMay, Former Chairman of the Military Joint Chiefs of Staff at the Pentagon.

Butch Blanchard

Senator Goldwater's letter to Lee M. Graham.

```
Mr. Lee M. Graham
526 West Maple
Monrovia, California 91016

Dear Mr. Graham:
First, let me tell you that I have long ago
give up acquiring access to the so-called Blue
Room at Wright-Patterson, as I have had one
long string of denials from chief after chief,
so I have give up. In answer to your questions,
"one is essentially correct." I don't know of
anyone who has access to the "Blue Room", nor
am I aware of its contents and I am not aware
of anything having been relocated. I can't
answer your question six, in fact, I can't find
anyone who would answer it.

To tell you the truth, Mr. Graham, "this thing
has gotten so highly classified," even though I
will admit there is a lot of it that has been
released, "it is just impossible to get
anything on it." I am returning your papers
because I know they are of value to you.
Sincerely,

Barry Goldwater
```

Note: Obtained through FOIA
Date Sent: 07-12-1986
Subject: 1983 Goldwater's letter.

*** *** ***

Senator Goldwater's letter to William S. Steinman.

Mr. William S. Steinman
15043 Rosalita Drive
La Mirada, California 90638

Dear Mr. Steinman:

To answer your questions, I have never gained
access to the so-called "Blue Room" at Wright
Patterson, so I have no idea what is in it.

I have no idea of who controls the flow of
"need-to-know" because, frankly, I was told in
such an emphatic way that it was none of my
business that I've never tried to made it my
business since.
I wish you luck on your investigation. I'm one
of those people who believe that with some two
billion planets scattered around our universe,
there has to be a couple of more that can
support life on it.

Sincerely,

Barry Goldwater

***   ***   ***

93

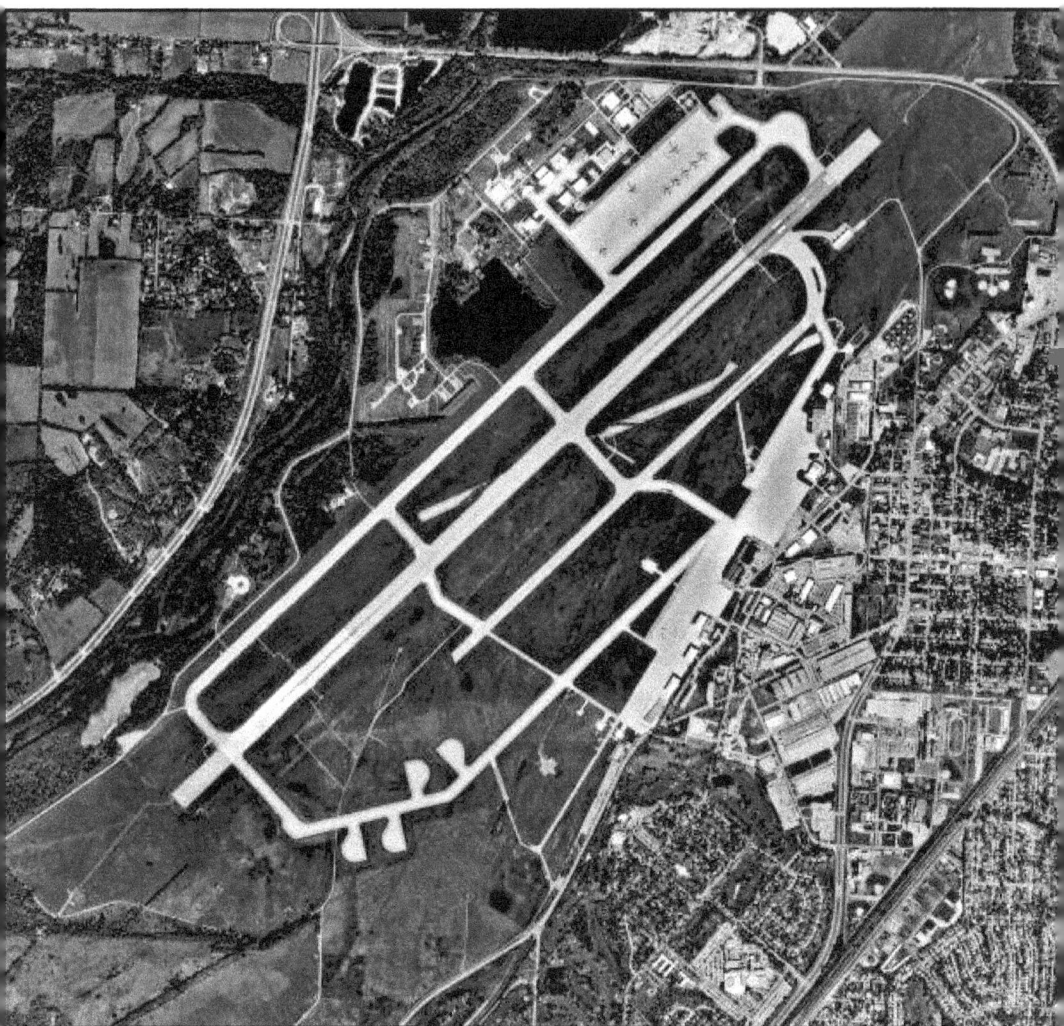

Wright-Patterson Air Force Base.

President Harry Truman-German UFOs Cover-up!

Why to coverup?
And the military aspect of UFOs' cover-up:
From day one, President Truman and the Pentagon did not want us to know a thing about UFOs. So for now, let's keep the NSA and the CIA on the back burner.

The President had multiple reasons to cover-up everything, while the military had only 3 reasons outlined as follows:
- 1-The UFOs are a purely "Military Secret", thus, the whole situation should remain exclusively under military jurisdiction and authority;
- 2-Preventing the Russians from knowing what the military knew about the German UFOs, and what the military was doing;
- 3-The military could not come up with a plausible explanation of what these UFOs were in reality, and how to reassure us that the UFOs were no danger to the American people.

Before February 1947, the United States military believed that UFOs were extraterrestrials. The OSS and the legendary Richard Helms concluded that the UFOs were German-made, and the Nazi and occult groups in Berlin and Munchen who had some sort of connection with extraterrestrials were an intricate part of the creation and development of UFOs, and other enigmatic flying machines.
In other words, the UFOs were part German, part extraterrestrial. For an extended period of time, top German scientists (Nazi or not Nazi) who were recruited by us would not talk about the *true* origin of the UFOs.
Some would say that the UFOs were German-made, others, like Dr. von Braun and Dr. Herman Oberth, reluctantly would admit that the German got help from extraterrestrials.
We have on record, a statement by Dr. Oberth which *de facto* ascertains that the German scientists got help from the aliens.

95

After April 1947, the military changed its opinion about the nature and origin of the UFOs, and became convinced that the UFOs of the era were the results of the research of Victor Schauberger, General Dr. Dornberger, Dr. von Braun, Alexander Lippisch, Dr. Richard Miethe, Karl Schapeller, SS General Jakob Sporrenberg, General Ernst Udet, Dr. Schumann, perhaps Maria Orsic, so on.
They based their original convictions on UFOs' patents registered in Germany, and drawings, maps and sketches of engines, machines, and crafts invented by Nazi scientists, such as, to name a few:
Lippisch aerodune,
Lippisch DM-1 (Delta Wing Plane),
Lippisch's supersonic and transcontinental bomber (Prototype of the Aurora),
Arthur Sack's circular flying machine,
The German ME 163,
Rudolph Schriever's technical data,
Alberto Fenoglio's sketches and blueprints,
The Horten 229,
Heinrich Focke 1939 patent of his VTOL HW Scnellflugzeug Rochen,
The sketches of the Geist Vril series,
Sketches of UFOs found in hangars in Letow, Breslaw and Dresden,
The notes of Karl Haushofer,
The interrogations of General Friedrich Wilhelm Müller,
The photos of the Andromeda Gerät,
The photos and technical data of the Rundflugzeug RFZ series (7 types),
The Haunebu series,
Schauberger's Repulsine and Repulsator, so on.

The UFOs were considered a "Military Secret":
In summary, the German UFOs were considered by the military as a top secret military affair, and consequently the American public, the media, as well as other intel and national security agencies should not know a thing about UFOs. Only the military should deal with UFOs.
It was a "Military Secret" and had nothing to do with politics.

General Hoyt S. Vandenberg

General Hoyt S. Vandenberg's intimidation and cover-up:

One of the master-minds of this theory was General Hoyt S. Vandenberg, a hero in his own right, and who was considered to be one of the most feared and powerful generals in American history. Probably, the General was right, taking into consideration that German UFOs were a "military secret". And military secrets should never be divulged. I totally agree with him. However, I totally disagree with General Vandenberg's tactics to deceive and even to intimidate all those (military, high ranking officers, scientists) who were assigned the duties to investigate German military technology and report on UFOs and distort the truth!

In my opinion, he was the architect *par excellence* of the most elaborate UFOs' cover-ups in military history.
Here is a brief synopsis of what he did.

In April 1948, intensive investigations and assessment of German UFOs, as well as recent UFOs' sightings reports were sent to General Vandenberg, for in that year, the General was in charge of everything related to UFOs.
The reports included very clear photos of the UFOs, new testimonies by German scientists, and witnesses' accounts (Pilots and military-men who saw the UFOs).
The General refused the reports and commented that the UFOs' sightings and the witnesses' accounts could and should not be taken seriously for lack of evidence.
In other words, he categorically rejected everything!
Why the General did not believe his own people?
And why did he discredit the professional assessment of military experts?
But did he? No, the General believed every word in the reports, but he wanted to crash all sorts of stories about UFOs, silence witnesses, and discourage anybody, including his own men from reporting any thing on UFOs! Furthermore, he instructed his people to describe the UFOs' sightings as hoaxes, to discredit and ridicule all those who report UFOs sightings.
In addition, he threatens captains, majors and colonels who pursue and authenticate UFOs sightings and credible reports, and let them know that they will be court-martialed!!

*** *** ***

Richard Helms

Note on Mr. Helms: Mr. Richard Helms did not share with President Truman what he knew about the German UFOs. And he had a good reason for not revealing secrets about the German UFOs, for he did not want the Russians to know a thing about the NAZI UFOs' program.
This is quite proper, legal and understandable.

***   ***   ***

President Harry S. Truman was the first and most informed American President on anything related to UFOs and aliens.

Harry Truman was the first American President to fully control the CIA, simply because he created the agency by signing the National Security Act of 1947, and after abolishing the OSS (Office of Strategic Services) and getting rid of General William Donovan, a protégé of President Franklin Roosevelt and former head of the OSS. The CIA was his baby.

President Truman was also the first and most informed American President on anything related to UFOs, intraterrestrials and extraterrestrial affairs, seconded only by President George Bush Sr., who served as Director of Central Intelligence from January 30, 1976 to January 20, 1977. (Replacing William Colby)
President Harry Truman was also the first American President to receive full report and detailed data on the German UFOs, Nazi exotic weapons, and Foo Fighters.

President Truman was delighted to see ufologists and a large portion of the general public spreading stories and allegations about aliens and extraterrestrial UFOs. The CIA warned him; he was told that the whole charade could backfire, but he did not give a damn. Insiders talked about how much President Truman distrusted the CIA. He learned and inherited "distrusting people and agencies" from his boss, President Roosevelt.
By the end of the forties and the beginning of the fifties, President Truman knew that he will be dealing with German UFOs, instead of extraterrestrial UFOs.

Harry Truman, Dwight Eisenhower and George Bush Sr. were vividly interested in the UFOs' question; but Truman was the first to create a protocol and procedures on how to initiate and conduct investigations, and gather information about UFOs.
President Truman allocated huge secret budgets for research on German UFOs, and how German flying saucers could be used militarily. However, by the end of his presidency, he lost interest in UFOs and aliens, who once he called "Space Monkeys"! But did he?
There are quite a few top secret Presidential memoranda signed by President Harry Truman, President Dwight Eisenhower and President Richard Nixon, which gave full authority to the CIA to disseminate information to confuse, disorient and misinform the Soviet Union.
In one of President Truman's secret memoranda, a reference was made to the aliens' influence and remnants of Nazi aerospace engineers' total control over strategic military points that could cause embarrassment to the United States Air Force, Navy and Army.

Nevertheless, the term "Alien Technology" was quickly and secretly replaced by "Nazi UFOs" and "German Technology."

Truman did not trust anybody.
He made it clear that these subjects should NOT be made public, communicated to the armed forces, and shared with other agencies.
He Okayed operations to uncover and investigate anything and everything related to German UFOs. He ordered the CIA to gather everything they could find, here and abroad on German UFOs, and investigate/assess OSS reports and findings on German technology and scientists.
By the same token, he specifically informed the agency that he is NOT interested in reading their reports on German UFOs and learning about their findings. (One of his deceptive tactics!)
He gave the agency carte blanche, with unlimited authority and power. He also authorized the agency to solicit the help of foreign agents, if necessary. The agency did. European spies, Russian operatives and British agents worked for the agency.
The agency recruited four former British code breakers, who cracked the code of the German Enigma Machine at the signals intelligence center at Bletchley Park in England.
In fact, two scientists from Poland were the first to unlock the complicated mechanism of Enigma, and decipher its codes, and not the Brits.
Alan Turing, was one of the first British code breakers who joined the agency's efforts to learn more about aliens symbols and codes. Again, the word "Aliens" was replaced by "German Technology".
On more than one occasion, President Truman told the head of the agency not to bother him anymore with UFOs/aliens' stuff.
In the same time, he made it clear to him, that nobody, no other agency, no one, not even the Air Force should know about this.
In other words, and simply put, the agency had to report to nobody, to no one!
Director of the FBI, Edgar J. Hoover and the military found out and were pissed off. Later on, when the Pentagon and the Air Force became heavily involved with UFOs, and took over the whole thing, Director Edgar J. Hoover wrote to them and asked to be permanently informed. In one of his letters he precisely showed an interest in the recovered dead bodies of three aliens.

The military ignored his request, and he went berserk.
But somehow, Hoover managed to get some very important documents from the intelligence agency.

Although President Truman gave full authority to the agency to take care of the German UFOs' business, secretly, he created his own committee to oversee what the agency was doing.
It is very ironic, because in a previous secret memo, and during a verbal communication with the director of the agency, President Truman made it clear to him that he is not interested in reading the reports and findings of the agency on UFOs and aliens (He called them "Space Monkeys!")

In fact, it is not so ironic, if you know a little bit about the character of President Truman.
He did it and said it on purpose, so he would and could legally and "honestly" deny any knowledge of the aliens, and UFOs.
He was protecting the "integrity of the office of the President of the United States."
Later on, it was found out that President Truman's intention was much broader. President Truman wanted to set the foundation of isolating any politician, any senator, any congressman, including future presidents from knowing anything about German UFOs. It seems bizarre, but it did happen.
His last communications with the Director of the agency would occur exclusively in the Oval Office, and only Marshall was allowed to be present.
Defense Secretary James V. Forrestal was barred from all the meetings.

*** *** ***

General William Donovan receiving a medal from President Harry Truman. And short after, Tuman fired Donovan. History repeats itself!

George Tenet, a former Director of the CIA receiving his medal from President George Bush. And short after Bush fired Tenet. History repeats itself! Mr. Tenet (A great patriot) was victimized!

From left to right: President Truman, Defense Secretary James V. Forrestal. President Truman got rid of Forrestal.

Did Secretary Forrestal commit suicide or was he killed?
Was he the first UFOs' cover-up victim?

On May 22, 1949, the ousted Forrestal committed suicide at the Bethesda Naval Hospital, Maryland, USA.
He was "quarantined" on the 16th floor suite, for psychiatric evaluation and intensive care. Report on his death as issued by the hospital stated that he jumped from a window in the 16th floor.
A very close associate of his said they killed him! The Secretary was taken by force to Bethesda Naval Hospital, on order from President Truman. And around the clock, 4 MP were guarding his room. A polite way to say, he was under a constant watch, not for his own safety, but to make sure that what was "planned" would be carried out without interference and suspicion.
Many believed Forrestal was the first official victim of German UFOs/Aliens Cover-up. The "AT Transcripts" did not make any reference to the suicide incident.

However, insiders could not keep their mouth shot; frustrated, they spread the rumors that hired operatives from a secret US agency closely related to the US military intelligence (Not the CIA) killed him and threw him out from the window.

*** *** ***

To set the record straight: Yes! They knew about German UFOs and their post-war secret bases.

During the Second World War, Germany was sending fleets of submarines, ships, and exotic spacecrafts (UFOs) to their unofficial colony, the Neu Schwabenland in the Antarctic, and to other secret locations and underground bases known only to Himmler, Kammler and to an elite of their military scientists.

Insiders, as well as United States and British intelligence confirmed that those underground secret bases were later used by the Germans after the war, as their new headquarters and center for their UFOs.

Files upon files confiscated by the allies at the secret German bases in the Harz Mountains, Thuringia and Peenemünde referred to the Antarctic's locations.

The OSS and United States military intelligence compiled lists and dossiers on highly advanced types and new classes of post-war German UFOs which were built at those locations.

In 1950, one of the CIA's secret memoranda revealed that in fact, a highly advanced type of German UFOs, as well as the UFOs seen over the United States and Europe came from the Antarctic's German new headquarters.

Photo: Allen Welsh Dulles.

In 1951, the Soviet Union and the United States secretly and jointly sent two expeditions to Antarctica to spy on post-war Germany's new UFOs' centers and underground factories in Neu Schwabenland.

105

The expeditions were mentioned in a secret CIA memorandum issued by General Walter Bedell Smith, then director of the CIA, and in a secret memorandum issued by Allen Welsh Dulles, then the Deputy Director of the Agency.

Photo: General Dr. Walter Dornberger.

In addition to the immense Neu Schwabenland's UFOs' centers, post-war Germany's scientists also established secret UFOs' factories in remote areas in Canada; this was confirmed by:
Dr. von Braun,
Major Erich Hatmann,
Erna Flegal,
Rudolph Schriever,
Dr. Hermann Oberth,
General Dr. Walter Dornberger,
Dr. Heinrich Richard Miethe,
Dr. Albert Kochendoerfer,
Dr. Bruno Wolf Bruckmann,
Robert Seamans (Associate NASA Administrator),
Walter Haeussemann (NASA Director of Astronics Division), Major General John Barclay, and of course, by Lt. Colonels Walter and Reimar Horten.

Some powerful people who were involved with the UFOs' question, reports, findings, disclosure and cover-ups.

Vital roles played, and extraordinary influence "imposed" to prevent full disclosure by some of those powerful personalities who remained totally unknown to ufologists, researchers, and the general public. To name a few:
Walter Bedell Smith, John R. Steelman, Allen Welsh Dulles, General Hoyt S. Vandenberg, and President Truman's National Defense Research Committe

Walter Bedell Smith

John R. Steelman

General John Samford played a major role in the Roswell's incident' coverup. He issued a ridiculous statement, but he was following orders.

General Roger Maxwell Ramey distorted the whole truth about the Roswell's incident. He was also following strict orders from The Pentagon.

General Curtis LeMay was the master-mind behind many UFOs/USOs' cover-ups. He was tough like steel.

President Harry Truman with members of the National Defense Research Committee: Roger Adams, Vannevar Bush, standing, third from left, K. T. Compton, James Bryant Conant, Alphonse Raymond, Albert Baird, Jerome Clarke, Frank B. Jewett, Alfred Newton, Lewis Hill, January 20, 1947.

The National Defense Research Committee played a major role in UFOs' cover-ups.

Amaat "A-Maat"; Anunnaki grand lord of the "liquid Energy":
Also known as "A-miat" referring to the Anunnaki goddess of water (Enki is the male god of Earth's water), that produced many life-forms at the dawn of the creation of our planet.
According to the Book of Ramadosh, "A-Maat", or water, gave birth to all living organisms in the oceans, seas and lands. Later on, it was discovered from extraterrestrial literature, that "A" or water was the primordial source of energy for the USOs (Unidentified Submerged Objects).

In pre-Islamic Arabic, as well as in contemporary literary and spoken Arabic, and Egyptian, the words "Maia", and "Mai" (Pronounced Maay) means water, and is directly derived from the Anunnaki language. As cited in the Koran, and as told by Mohammad, Miat or Maia was source of all life-forms and life in general. It is written in the Koran and ancient Islamic scriptures: "Wa Khalkna Lakum min al mai, koula shay en hay."
Translated verbatim: "And we have created for you, from the water, everything that is alive."
Worth mentioning here, that many of the early Islamic scholars called "Al Allamah" (a variation of Ulema), were familiar with the teachings and writings of the Anunnaki-Ulema.
In their book "Ilmu Al Donia" (Knowledge of the Universe), the Anunnaki-Ulema wrote: "A-miat created the Earth, the animals, the plants and the humans."
Later on, the Babylonians will adopt this primordial concept, and incorporate it in their clay tablets. The word "A" appeared in Sumerian, Akkadian, and Assyrian languages, and meant water.
According to the Assyriologist Dr. Hinck, "A" also meant river, and sounded "pur", as in Purrat.
Originally, it was written phonetically, and was used in plural form, and the Assyrian word Miat became associated with its original meaning (Water). Tiglath Pileser said: *"A-na mie inadu",* meaning "into waters shall I cast."
Sennacherib said: "Miat-su nadi kazuti a-na zumme-ya lu asti," meaning "Of its flowing nauseous waters for my thirst I drank."
And in the Anunnaki Book of Rama-Dosh, Sinhar Marduck said: "An-i miat, rafat bashar-ji," meaning: "From its water, I elevated (created) Bashar (Man, human race)."

In the ancient Assyrian language, "A" meant water of the gods; rain. Legend has it that the monarchs of ancient Mesopotamia, Sumer and Babylon avoided at all costs to walk under the rain in a battle, because they believed that doing so will anger the gods, and bring bad luck.

Sennacherib said: "Unnu va salgu nahli nathu saddi adura", meaning: "Rain and snow, torrents, clefts of mountains, I avoided."

The Akkadian/Sumerian tablets, as well as the Anunnaki's scrolls revealed that "A" gave birth to a great Anunnaki goddess called "Lady Plant", Ninsar in Akkadian, Sumerian and old Babylonian.

In conclusion, the Anunnaki goddess "A" was the origin of the Hebrew, Christian and Muslim belief in the ritual purification of the body through water.

Amchit: Phoenician. Noun. Pronounced Amcheet.
Name of an ancient Phoenician town of Jbeil (Ancient Byblos) in Lebanon. Amchit sits on the Lebanese coast and climbs gently to the lower plateau of Mount Lebanon. It is a very beautiful town known for the exquisite architecture of its ethnic and traditional homes, and the legendary hospitality of its people.

French Orientalists called Amchit paradise on earth. The French archaeologist and writer, Ernest Renan, who lived there with his sister Henriette (Buried in Amchit) mentioned this splendid town in one of his writings.

He wrote: "We admit, me, my wife and my sister that Amchit is a paradise". Amchit is rich with archeological and historical sites; its Church of Saint Sophia is built on the ruins of a Phoenician foundation; the Church of Saint Zakhia, which goes back to the 6th century; the famous church of Lady of Saydet Naya built by the Crusaders. Unquestionably, Amchit is one of the most beautiful spots on earth.

Amenophis IV (Akhenaton): In an Egyptian Hymn to the Sun-God, written circa 1,400 B.C., we read that the Sun-God is "The primordial Being, who himself made himself...the one and only God..." It is very clear that we are reading here a declaration of monotheism. It is documented that monotheism was introduced into Egypt by Amenophis IV, who called God Aton the "only God, the one, supreme, and only God."

111

Amchit

Amchit, Lebanon.

Amenophis IV

This was expressed in an Egyptian hymn in praise to God Aton. The hymn was translated and published in "Breasted's Development of Religion and Thoughts in Ancient Egypt."

In section 65 of the hymn we read: "O Sole God, whose powers no others (Other gods) have (Possessed). In section 110, we read, "Thou alone shining in thy form as living Aton." In section 120, we read, "There is no other that knoweth Thee."

No doubt, the Egyptian Hymn deeply influenced Psalm 104. Refer to "The Treasury of Ancient Egypt" by Weigall, published in London in 1911.

Yahwehism was not the product of divine revelations to Abraham and to Moses while he was wandering in the Sinai Desert, according to 1 Kings 6:1 (Circa 1446 B.C.)

Archaeological excavations proved beyond the shadow of a doubt, that there is no presence of a Late Bronze Age in the Sinai Desert and at Mount Sinai (Jabal Mousa).

And the fact that the Hebrews (Israelites) names at that period in time and long after the alleged Exodus kept the theophoric "Yaw", is a strong indication that they retained their polytheistic beliefs and worship of several gods, simply because polytheism was their original religious heritage and their primordial social-religious beliefs-system.

Amioun: The name of an old town in Lebanon.
Amioun's history goes back to the time of the Phoenicians. Amioun was mentioned as Amia in the 14th century B.C. Letters of Tel Al Amarna, written by Phoenician kings who were subjects of the pharaoh.
Epistemologically, the word Amioun derived from the Aramaic word Emun, which means fortress.
In 1946, in the vicinity of the tower of St. Phocas in Amioun, engineers members of the French military topography team discovered unidentified ancient parchments, figurines, Assyrian coins, tablets, slabs, and Phoenician terracotta-clay fragments containing passages from the Phoenician story of the Creation, and a substantial deposit of minted gold.
Amioun's history goes back to the time of the Phoenicians.

Amioun was mentioned as Amia in the 14th century B.C. Letters of Tel Al Amarna, written by Phoenician kings who were subjects of the pharaoh. Epistemologically, the word Amioun derived from the Aramaic word Emun, which means fortress.
In 1946, in the vicinity of the tower of Saint Phocas in Amioun, engineers members of the French military topography team discovered unidentified ancient parchments, figurines, Assyrian coins, tablets, slabs, and Phoenician terracotta-clay fragments containing passages from the Phoenician story of the Creation, and a substantial deposit of minted gold.

*** *** ***

Amioun, Lebanon.

Amnesia (Doorway Amnesia): A temporary laps of memory. However, ufologists use it as a term to refer to cases when an abductee is unable to remember when, and how he/she entered an extraterrestrial craft against his/her will.

Amrit: A Phoenician/Ugaritic noun.
Name of an ancient Phoenician city located in Syria, built by both the remnants of the Anunnaki, and the early Phoenicians from Tyre and Sidon. Amrit is derived from the Ana'kh Ammr-il.

The remains of the Phoenician Temple of Melkart at Amrit.

Amrit is one of the most puzzling, mysterious and enigmatic cities in recorded history.

It was the stage for a cosmic war between many ancient nations; the birth of the original Olympiads; the world's first Anunnaki-Phoenician medical center; the city that produced Mah-Rit, the early form/formula of what we today call steroids, an early genetic product created by the Anunnaki.

Melkart of Carthage.

The Melkart's Shrines at Carthage (Modern Tunis) and Amrit were decorated with Anunnaki motifs and symbols, such as the Arwad Serpent representing wisdom, knowledge and science, and the Tyrian moon crescent, representing new birth, and the Anunnaki Delta-Tyrian Triangle, representing the equilibrium of nature and man.

Ruins of the Phoenician cemetery of Amrit.

Around this ancient Phoenician monument, the ritual ceremony of Mahrit took place.

Today, tourists visiting Amrit are fascinated by an elaborate altar built by the Phoenicians, to honor their god Melkart (A god created for the Phoenicians by the Anunnaki). But in fact, the altar was erected by the remnants of the Anunnaki, who had an influential center on the Island of Arwad, not very far from Amrit. The altar served as a healing center using Anunnaki medicine, and Phoenician oracles.

Amrit was a scientific center for the remnants of the Anunnaki, and early Phoenicians who practiced a very advanced form of medicine mixed, with oracles and parapsychological powers.

The Crusaders, and particularly the Knights Templar, organized secret meetings on the plateau of the temple, and read excerpts from the Book of Rama Dosh, especially the passages related to metal transmutation, that allowed them to change iron and copper into gold.

Sepulchral monuments at Amrit.

An: Sumerian/Chaldean. Noun.
Name of the chief god of the Annunaki.
Anu in Egyptian
Anum in Akkadian.
An was the creator of the gods, including the peoples of the earth,
but over time (3000-2500 B.C.) An lost his privileged position to
his son Enlil.
His main temple was in Uruk, where he was worshipped as the god
of that city. Later on, his daughter Inanna became a co-god of
Uruk. An mated with the goddesses Ki and Nammu.
His union with them gave birth to the gods.

In Sumerian, "An" means:
a- Sky.
b- High.
The word "An" was commonly used by Hurrians, Phoenicians,
Elamites, Subarians, Sumerians, Akkadians, Medes, and Kasites.
See Anum

Illustration of Anum (An, Anu) as chief of the Anunnaki.

Subjects bringing dates (Palm dates/fruits) to Anu.
God Anu

God An (Anu).

"An", or "Anu", chief god of the Annunaki.
A scene depicting an offering to Anu.

By comparing the size of god Anu to the size of his subject, Anu clearly appears as a giant. In fact, Anu and his Anunnaki's legions were called "Gibborim", "Gababira" (Giants) by the early Hebrews and the Bible's scribes, as well as by the Phoenicians, Hittites, Sumerians and Mesopotamians. The Anunnaki's star is carved on the very top of the slab/cylinder, a reminder/symbol of the celestial origin of the Anunnaki.

All subjects and worshipers before Anu were always depicted as small persons, to reflect the gigantic status of the Anunnaki god, on so many levels, including supreme authority, domination of Earth, and the origin of civilizations on Earth.

"An" or "Anu", the celestial father, and supreme god of the Anunnaki.

An-Hayya'h, "A-haYA", "Aelef-hayat": Ana'kh/Ulemite.
An-Hayya'h could be the most important word in the whole literature of the Anunnaki and Ana'kh, because it deals with:
1-The origin of man on earth;
2-How humans are connected to the Anunnaki;
3-Importance of water vis-à-vis humans and Anunnaki;
4-The life of humans;
5-Proof that it was a non-terrestrial woman who created man, Adam and the human race via her Anunnaki identity;
6-The return of the Anunnaki to earth;
7-Humanity salvation, hopes, and a better future for all of us; "a gift from our ancestors and creators, the Anunnaki," said the Ulema.
It is extremely difficult to find the proper and accurate word or words in our terrestrial languages and vocabularies.
The word "An-Hayya'h" is composed of:
1-An or A (Pronounced Aa), or Aelef (Pronounced a'leff).
It is the same letter in Ana'kh, Akkadian, Canaanite, Babylonian, Assyrian, Ugaritic, Phoenician, Moabite, Siloam, Samaritan, Lachish, Hebrew, Aramaic, Nabataean-Aramaic, Syriac, and Arabic. All these languages are derived from the Ana'kh.
(Note: The early Greeks adopted the Phoenician Alphabet, and the Latin and Cyrillic came from the Greek.
The Hebrew, Aramaic and Greek scripts all came from the Phoenician. Arabic and most of Indian scriptures came from the Aramaic. The entire Western world received its languages from the Phoenicians, the descendants of the Anunnaki.)
An means one or all of the following:
1-Beginning;
2-The very first;
3-The ultimate;
4-The origin;
5-Water.
On earth, this word became Alef in Phoenician, Aramaic, Hebrew, Syriac and Arabic. Alef is the beginning of the alphabet in these languages.
In Latin, it's A, and in Greek is Alpha.

125

In Hebrew, the Aleph consists of two yuds (Pronounced Yood); one Yud is situated to the upper right and the other yud to the lower left.

Both Yuds are joined by a diagonal *vav*. They represent the higher water and the lower water, and between them the heaven. This mystic-kabalistic interpretation was given to us by Rabbi Isaac Luria.

Water is extremely important in all the sacred scriptures, as well as in the vast literature and scripts of extraterrestrials and Anunnaki. Water links humans to the Anunnaki.

In the Babylonian account of the Creation, Tablet 1 illustrates Apsu (Male), representing the primeval fresh water, and Tiamat (Female), the primeval salt water.

These were the parents of the gods. Apsu and Tiamat begat Lahmu (Lakhmu) and Lahamu (Lakhamu) deities.

In the Torah, the word water was mentioned in the first day of the creation of the world: "And the spirit of God hovered over the surface of the water." In the Chassidut, the higher water is "wet" and "warm", and represents the closeness to Yahweh (God), and it brings happiness to man.

The lower water is "cold", and brings unhappiness because it separates us from Yahweh (God), and man feels lonely and abandoned. The Ten Commandments commences with the letter Alef: "Anochi (I) am God your God who has taken you out of the land of Egypt, out of the house of bondage."

The letter Alef holds the secret of man, his creation and the whole universe (Midrash).

In Hebrew, the numeric value of Aleph is 1. And the meaning is:
1-First;
2-Adonai;
3-Leader;
4-Strength;
5-Ox;
6-Bull;
7-Thousand;
8-To teach.

According to Jewish teaching, each Hebrew letter is a spiritual force and power by itself, and comes directly from Yahweh (God).

This force contains the raw material for the creation of the world and man. The Word of God ranges from the Aleph (The very first letter) to the Tav (The last letter) in Hebrew.

In Revelation 1:8, Jesus said: "I am Alpha and Omega, the beginning and the ending."

In John 1:1-3, as the Word becomes Jesus, the Lord Jesus is also the Aleph and the Tav, as well as the Alpha and the Omega. In Him exists all the forces, and spiritual powers of the creation. Jesus is also connected to water, an essential substance for the purification of the body and the soul, this is why Christians got to be baptized in water.

In Islam, water is primordial and considered as the major force of the creation of the universe.

The Prophet Mohammad said (From the Quran): "Wa Khalaknah Lakoum min al Ma'i, koula chay en hay", meaning: And WE (Allah) have created for you from water everything alive."

The Islamic numeric/spiritual value of Aleph and God is 1.

To the Anunnaki and many extraterrestrial civilizations, the An or Alef represents number 1, as well as planet Nibiru, the constellation Orion, the star Aldebaran, and above all the female aspect of the creation symbolized in the Anunnaki's female "Gb'r" (Angel Gabriel to us.)

2-Hayya'h also means:

a-Life;

b-Creation;

c-Humans;

d-Earth.

In Arabic, Hebrew, Aramaic, Turkish, Syriac, and so many Eastern languages, the Anunnaki words "Hayya'h" and "Hayat" mean the same thing: Life.

But the most striking part of our story is that the original name of Eve is not Eve, but "Hawwa" derived directly from Hayya. How do we know this? Very simple: Eve's name in the Bible is "Hawwa", also "Chevvah".

In the Quran is also "Hawwa", and in all the Semitic and Akkadian texts, Eve is called Hawwa or Hayat, meaning the giver of life; the source of the creation.

Now, if we combine the 2 words: An +Hayya'h or Hayat, we get this: Beginning; The very first; The ultimate; The origin; Water +

Life; Creation; Humans; Earth, where the first was created; Woman.

And the whole meaning becomes: The origin of the creation and first thing or person who created the life of humans was a woman (Eve; Hawwa) or water.

Amazingly enough, in Ana'kh, woman and water mean the same thing, because woman as a creative female energy represents water according to the Babylonian, Sumerians and Anunnaki tablets, as clearly written in the Babylonian-Sumerian account of the Creation, Tablet 1.

The Anunnaki who created us genetically some 65,000 B.C. lived on earth with us, in Iraq (Sumer, Mesopotamia, Babylon) and Lebanon (Loubnan, Phoenicia, Phinikia).

They taught our ancestors how to write, how to speak, how to play music, how to build temples, how to navigate, as well as geometry, algebra, metallurgy, irrigation, astronomy, you name it. But the human races disappointed them, for the early human beings were cruel, violent, greedy and ungrateful.

So, the Anunnaki gave up on us and left earth.

The few remaining Anunnaki living in Iraq and Lebanon were killed by savage military legions from Greece, Turkey and other nations of the region. The Anunnaki left earth for good.

Other extraterrestrial races came to earth, but these celestial visitors were not friendly and considerate like our ancestors the Anunnaki.

The new extraterrestrials had a different plan for humanity, and their agenda included abduction of women and children, animal mutilation, genetic experiments on human beings, creating a new hybrid race, etc...

The Anunnaki did not totally forget us. After all, many of their women were married to humans, and many of our women were married to Anunnaki.

Ancient history, the Bible, Sumerian tablets, Akkadian cylinders, Babylonian scriptures, Phoenician inscriptions, and historical accounts from around the globe recorded these events.

You can find them, almost intact, in archeological sites in Iraq and Lebanon, as well as in museums, particularly the British Museum, the Iraqi Museum and the Lebanese Museum.

So, before leaving us, the Anunnaki activated in our cells the infinitesimally invisible multimicroscopic gene of An-Hayya'h.

It was implanted in our organism and became a vital composition of our DNA.

Humans are not yet aware of this, as we were not aware of the existence of our DNA for thousands of years.

As our medicine, science and technology advance, we will be able one day to discover that miniscule, invisible, undetectable An-Hayya'h, exactly as we have discovered our DNA. An-Hayya'h cannot be detected yet in our laboratories.

It is way beyond our reach and our comprehension.

It is extremely powerful, because it is the very source of our existence.

Through An-Hayya'h, the Anunnaki remained in touch with us, even though we are not aware of it. It is linked directly to a Conduit and to a Miraya (Monitor, or mirror) on Nibiru. Every single human being on the face of the earth is linked to the outer-world of the Anunnaki through An-Hayya'h. And it is faster than the speed of light. It reaches the Anunnaki through Babs (Star gates).

For now, we will call it molecule or bubble. This molecule travels the universe and reaches the Miraya of the Anunnaki through a Conduit integrated in our genes and our brain's cells by the Anunnaki some 65,000 years ago. But what is a Conduit?

Does every human possess a Conduit?

The answer is yes.

All humans have a Conduit just like the Anunnaki, because it is part of our DNA. It is impossible to explain how a Conduit works inside the human brain, and/or how it works for a human being.

The creation of the Conduit is the most important procedure done for each Anunnaki's student on the first day of his or her entrance into a learning center in Ashtari.

A new identity is created for each Anunnaki's student by the development of a new pathway in his or her mind, connecting the student to the rest of the Anunnaki's psyche.

Simultaneously, the cells check with the other copy of the mind and body of the Anunnaki student, to make sure that the Double and the other copy of the mind and body of the student are totally clean.

During this phase, the Anunnaki's student temporarily loses his or her memory, for a very short time.

This is how the telepathic faculty is developed, or enhanced in everyone. It is necessary, since to serve the total community of the Anunnaki, the individual program inside each Anunnaki's student is immediately shared with everybody.

The Anunnaki have two kinds of intelligence:

1-Collective intelligence that belongs to the community.

2-Individual intelligence that belongs to one person.

Both intelligences are directly connected to two things:

1-The first is the access to the Community Depot of Knowledge that any Anunnaki can tap in and update and acquire additional knowledge.

2-The second is an individual prevention shield, also referred to as personal privacy.

This means that an Anunnaki can switch on and off his/her direct link to other Anunnaki. By establishing the Screen or Filter an Anunnaki can block others from either communication with him or her, or simply prevent others from reading personal thoughts.

Filter, Screen and Shield are interchangeably used to describe the privacy protection device.

In addition, an Anunnaki can program telepathy and set it up on chosen channels, exactly as we turn on our radio set and select the station we wish to listen to. Telepathy has several frequency, channels and stations. When the establishment of the Conduit is complete, the student leaves the conic cell, where the procedure has taken place, and heads to the classroom.

Now, how does an Anunnaki receive the content of a Conduit to allow him/her to watch over us?

Through the Miraya (See Miraya to learn how it works).

The Anunnaki created the Conduit, the Miraya and the An-Hayya'h to watch over us, even though we do not deserve it, said the Ulema. The Anunnaki have been watching us, monitoring our activities, listening to our voices, witnessing our wars, brutality, greed and indifference toward each others for centuries.

But they did not interfere. But now, they will, because they fear two things that could destroy earth and annihilate the human race:

1-The domination of earth and the human race by the Greys;

2-The destruction of human life and planet Earth on the hands of humans.

The whole earth could blow up. Should this happen, the whole solar system could be destroyed.

For we know, should anything happen to the moon, the earth will cease to exist. This is an absolute truth and a fact accepted by all scientists. So anything that could happen to earth will disrupt the solar system, said the Ulema. An-Hayya'h is our umbilical cord, our birth cord that attaches us to the Anunnaki. Some refer to it as the "Silver Chord".

No matter how silly and crazy this concept might look to many of us, one day, we will accept and possibly we might understand its mind-boggling mysteries, when our science, technology and mind explore wider dimensions, and reach a higher level of cosmic awareness and intelligence, added the Ulema.

Farid Tayarah said: "An-Hayya'h will always be there for you to use before you depart this earth. It will never go away, because it is part of you. Without it you couldn't exist. Just before you die, your brain out of the blue wills activate it for you."

Ana'kh: Language of the Anunnaki and the extraterrestrials from Aldebaran who descended on Sumeria and Phoenicia according to the Anunnaki Ulema. Part of the Ana'kh language lexicon is preserved in the Book of Ramadosh, and Book Ilmu Al Donia.

Ulema Albakr stated that Ana'kh was used by the early human beings who lived on the Island of Arwad, in Tyre, Sidon and Byblos.

Albakr added, "From the Ana'kh derived the primitive languages of the Near East and the Middle East." Many words in Hebrew, Aramaic, Syriac, Coptic, Phoenician, Akkadian, Hittite, Babylonian, Urdu, Mesopotamian, Sumerian, Arabic, Hungarian, Egyptian, Armenian, Enochean, Nabatean, and Aramean derived from the Anakh. Ana'kh sounds Semitic, because of its phonetics. But it is "not Semitic at all", said Ulema Ghandar Gupta. It has no grammar, but has an extremely rich vocabulary and an abundance of metaphoric expressions. A considerable number of Akkadian and Sumerian words that appeared in th eMesopotamian Epic of Creation derived from the Ana'kh.

Around 569 A.D., a group of Ulema in the Near East (Non-Islamic scholars) compiled an extensive list of Ana'kh words and phrases.

In 625, A.D., two leading figures of the Ulema brotherhood wrote the Book of Ramadosh; a compilation of Ana'kh terminology, a lexicon, and Kiraats (Readings). Ulema Albakr stated that the Ulema is not a religious group, and they are not Muslim.

In fact, they were persecuted by the companions of the Prophet Muhammad, and were expelled from the Arab Peninsula. They found refuge in Cyprus, Malta and Marseille. But he was quick to point out that the early Sufi masters, poets and Sufi trance dancers were Ulema. He added "The Ulema should not be confused with the Islamic Ulema who teach Islamic law, or with the Allamah who were the leading Islamic figures of science and letters in medieval times."
Farid Tayarah, an Ulema himself, and a former head of a Masonic Lodge stated that the Ana'kh was used during Middle Eastern Masonic sessions.

Anakim: Sumerian/Akkadian/Hebrew. Noun.
The descendants of Anak, or Enoch, Cain's son. Although it was claimed by Biblical scholars, and particularly by the Hebrew scribes that a flood had been sent to destroy the Anakim, there were still entire cities and settlements of Anakim in the lands of Canaan as late as the time of Moses.
Jewish chronicler Josephus wrote that even in his own day it was not uncommon for people to dig up gigantic skeletal remains, referring to the giant Anakim.
Spies sent by Moses to report on the Anakim's strongholds reported back that the Anakim were so large that the Hebrews seemed "like grasshoppers" in comparison.

Analog model for linearized general relativity: Science describes linearized turbulent fluid as analog model for linearized general relativity, in other words, gravity-electro-magnestism. Some ufologists have claimed that this sciemtific concept applies to UFOs' reverse engineering program carried at Area 51.

Anamesis Project: According to the Greek philosopher Plato, the acquisition of knowledge is pragmatically remembering what we already know.

The Anamesis Project was created in Austria, by Dr. Alex Keul, in order to gather the parapsychological elements and factors of UFOs' experiences, upon interviewing witnesses of UFOS' sightings.

Anamidra:
I. Definition and introduction
II. Anamidra and Earth Matrix.
III. Anamidra explains what kind of clay the Anunnaki used to create Man.
IV. Anamidra explains the creation of Man from cosmic clay.

I. Definition and introduction:
Anamidra is the name of the Anunnaki scientist who monitors the Earth Matrix, known as Anamid-Raya, also Anid Ariya.
This Matrix is extremely complicated, because it is written in codes, symbols, geometrical forms, chemical formulas, theorems, "and in all the languages that have existed, still exist, and will be invented in the future after 2022," said the Ulema.
In other words, it is a cosmic library, archive, and depository of all the knowledge and events of 5 billion years, the estimated date of the beginning of Earth.

II. Anamidra and Earth Matrix:
Anamidra provided fascinating and mind-bending information on this matrix that has captivated academicians and leading scientists in the Eastern and Western hemispheres. Included in his data are detailed descriptions and explanations of:
- 1-Primordial bio-engineering of terrestrial life-forms (Elements, nature, animals, and humans);
- 2-Building blocks of life, and how they acted like cells to produce life on earth;
- 3-DNA's fifth unknown element;
- 4-RNA (Human and non-human) and life evolution;
- 5-The origin and the genetic creation of the human races by the Anunnaki;

- 6-The Earth-made human creatures;
- 7-The Space-made human creatures;
- 8-Metabolism and the oceans-made human creatures;
- 9-Man-made humans and reverse engineering of the human brain;
- 10-The Anunnaki's "Conduit".

III. Anamidra explains what kind of clay the Anunnaki used to create Man:

One of the most striking revelations of Sinhar Anamidra is his explanation of the "Clay" used by the Anunnaki to genetically create the first human species.

The Anunnaki's matrix mentioned clay as one of the primordial ingredients or elements they have used to create the human race. It is extremely important to understand the real meaning of the word clay. Anamidra explained to the Ulema, that "Clay" is not what everybody understood or thought it to be, from reading the translations of the Sumerian texts.

It is not the earthly clay found in ancient Sumer near the Tigris and Euphrates banks. The Anunnaki's matrix explained and defined it very differently.

Judaism, Christianity and Islam got hooked on clay. Scholars who have translated the Sumerian texts and/or interpreted them, made a huge mistake when they referred to clay as the mud or dirt substance the Anunnaki found in ancient Iraq, and then mixed it with their DNA to create mankind..." said Ulema Govinda.

The Anunnaki used a plasmic liquid that coagulated very rapidly, and shortly thereafter, the coagulation took the apparent physical properties of the clay. But the substance was not dirt, rather it was a plasmo-organic substance.

Anamidra told the Ulema, that some of the very early human races were not created by the Anunnaki. The earliest human-animal species were originally created in space, and this included many animals and various plants. And by that he meant that life of the earliest human-animal species started within the clay found inside of comets.

IV. Anamidra spoke about the early human species who lived underwater:

Anamidra spoke to the Anunnaki-Ulema about the existence and origin of early human-like creatures who lived at the bottom of the oceans. He explained that one of the earliest life-forms on planet Earth, began at the very bottom of the oceans, where metabolism originated through "Mai-ai" (Water)
Metabolism created an early human-like form. These creatures had a human skull, two eyes without retina, two legs and four long arms, but no nose, no ears, and no hair on their bodies." They were called the Basharma'h. (Bashar means human race, and Ma'h means water.)

Ana Noura of Ashtari (Aldebaran):
Also called Ambar Ana.Ti.
Name of the wife of a high-ranking Anunnaki, an earth woman who is a direct descendant of the Phoenician Anunnaki race, and who came forward to reveal new and astounding information about many subjects that have, until now, been top secret.
The woman, who is known only by her first name, was born on earth and adopted by a prominent family. A brilliant woman, she attended one of the best universities in the Northeast and became a successful business woman, but through unforeseen events had been approached by a high ranking Anunnaki with the request to bear a child. At age sixty, when shewas ready to return to Ashtari (Aldebaran) to be rejuvenated and prepared for a lifespan of hundreds of thousands of years, she decided to give the benefit of her experience to humanity. Ambar Ana.Ti approached me with her request to publish her story.

Her letter in Aramaic-Assyrian:
"After much soul-searching, I have decided to write to you.
Because of my unique experience, I have read many books about the Anunnaki, but your book, *The Anunnaki's Genetic Creation of the Human Race* was the one nearest the truth, and I appreciated its spirit of investigation and non-judgmental attitude. However, there is much in there which is incorrect. The wrong material was based on articles and statements of American Ufologists, and unfortunately, they lack the necessary knowledge. Allow me to give you an example.

Most of the people who claim to have met the aliens describe them as three to four feet tall, gray, and possessing big, dark, bug eyes. This is not the case.

Some of the aliens do, indeed, answer to this description, but generally they do not, and often they look just like us since they are shape changers. When the alien appears to you, the first thing you notice is dusty light with tiny particles in it. Soon the particles begin to coagulate, to form a center, and suddenly you see the form of small baby.

Then, an explosion-like phenomenon occurs, and the shape changes to a grown human, but it is deformed, as if still adjusting itself. For example, his back may overlap his neck, or part of his hips extends far from his body.

That lasts a few minutes, and then the shape rearranges itself into a perfectly normal human. You may wonder how I know, maybe even think I am being arrogant and unreasonable. But this is not so. My certainty is based upon my personal relationship with the Anunnaki, and particularly, with the one who is, to all intents and purposes, my husband, even if our marriage ceremony was non-traditional. I would also like to note that my alien husband does not object to my revelations. In fact, since the year 2022 is almost upon us (and I don't have to tell you the significance of this year) he feels the time has come to be more open about the relationship between humans and extraterrestrials.

The first time the alien appeared to me, many years ago, his eyes looked like glittering light. I could not take my own eyes off them, and could not move, as if I were hypnotized. Then, his eyes calmed down, became normal, and immediately I felt I could move again. Another claim which I did not find to be true is that the aliens speak to us telepathically.

It was nothing of the sort with me. The alien spoke, but that was even stranger than telepathy, because at first he sounded like an old record that was played at the wrong speed – fast, squeaky, scratching. Then the sound adjusted, and the voice became a normal human voice. A very pleasant human voice.

What really upsets me, though, is the idea that all aliens are out to rape, mutilate, and generally harm their abductees. This was not the case with me – exactly the opposite.

I have never met such respect, such gentleness, such willingness to accommodate the other person, in any human being. Nor was I abducted in the sense that anything was done against my wishes.

True, I was asleep in my bed, and I woke up in a strange place, but as soon as I got out of my strange inability to move, and Sinhar Marduchk adjusted his voice, he immediately reassured me I was a guest, that I could go home any minute I chose to, and that all he wanted was to tell me certain things he felt I should know. I could see no reason to object, seeing here was an opportunity to learn so much, and that no harm would come to me.

Besides, Marduchk was so incredibly handsome and charming, I rather enjoyed his companionship and did not see any reason to cut my visit short.

Therefore, I expressed my gratitude for the invitation, and was ready to listen. The first thing Sinhar Marduchk told me, after introducing himself, was indeed a shock. He informed me that I am a descendant of the Phoenician-Anunnaki! That I am really and truly one of them. While shocking, it made a strange sort of sense.

You see, Mr. de Lafayette, I did not really know my birth parents. I was adopted in infancy by a wonderful couple who made excellent parents and loved me very much. I would have known I was adopted even if they had not told me, because here I was with olive skin, black hair, and dark brown eyes, while my parents, who came from England, were both blond.

When I expressed a wish, as a teenager, to find out who my birth parents were, they tried to help, but we did not have much luck, so I gave up. All the information was locked up and unavailable.

Therefore, when my new alien friend informed me that my ancestry went back to the relationship between the early Anunnaki and the "daughters of men," I was shocked, but not for long.

Apparently, I was born in Iraq, and my birth parents were Ashurians, who are Middle Eastern Christians, related to the Syriac, who still speak Aramaic among themselves.

"Would you like to speak your own language?" asked Sinhar Marduchk, smiling, his large, black, Anunnaki eyes full of humor.

"Of course," I said.

"But it would probably take years to learn, right?"

"Wrong," said Sinhar Marduchk. He looked into my eyes, and his own eyes started acting as before, with the hypnotic glittering light. I felt paralyzed again, but only for a few seconds. Then it stopped, I shook myself, and to my utter disbelief found myself talking and understanding a language that I have never heard before.

"Will I forget it as soon as I go home?" I asked.

"No, it is my gift to you. You can now read it, too." I was thrilled. From then on we always speak Aramaic between us.

Anyway, I have so much to tell you, Mr. de Lafayette, so possibly my own story is of less importance than the revelations and knowledge I acquired from my new friends and family.

The Anunnaki live for thousands of years, and their understanding of history is very deep. We, who live such short lives, make many historical mistakes, even when written records are available. Take, for instance, the issue of Jesus and the crucifixion. I was raised a Presbyterian, and my parents took me quite often to church. It had become a habit and I never questioned or even thought about the Crucifixion. Well, imagine my surprise when Sinhar Marduchk told me that Jesus did not die on the cross!

I hope I am not upsetting anyone, but the real story involves the existence of two tombs. Apparently, two disciples planned it all out with Jesus' mother and with his wife, Mary Magdalene. One of them gave Jesus a rag soaked in something that made him sleep.

Later in the day he was indeed stabbed with a spear, but not fatally, and at sunset the soldiers assumed he was dead and took him down.

The two disciples that had arranged the matter wrapped him with a shroud, and took him to a faraway cave to hide him and help him recover, but then they took the bloody shroud and left it in the tomb everyone expected him to be in.

He was never there, and in the morning, the other disciples, or anyone else interested in him, assumed he left the tomb and left the shroud there, thus giving rise to the story of the resurrection.

They took Jesus secretly to Phoenicia, where he fully recovered, then put him and his wife on a Phoenician boat that went to Cyprus.

Eventually, they fled to Marseille, where they settled permanently and had children.

Jesus worked in his profession, a handyman (he never really was a carpenter, this is a translation mistake), lived peacefully, and avoided all matters of religion for the rest of his life.

His descendants lived in France, and perhaps some of them still exist, I really don't know.

"Does that story bother you?" asked Sinhar Marduchk. "Not at all," I said. "I am no longer a religious person, and I would much rather know the truth than live in ignorance." Sinhar Marduchk smiled with appreciation. Apparently he liked to see that I kept an open mind. I must tell how I was later rewarded by being taught how to time travel, and thus be able to meet Mary Magdalene and Jesus in person.

Also, another major revelation about other great religions such as Islam, Sinhar Marduchk told me that the Koran, the holy book I really admire and respect, did not descend on Muhammad from Heaven, but he learned it from a Christian ascetic monk in the desert.

This monk was known in the area as "Raheb Bouhayrah" meaning, priest, or monk, of the lake. After all, Muhammad could not read and write, as is well known. He had to remember by heart what the priest told him on a weekly basis.

Probably you are not very religious, and will not pay attention to these details, but would you be interested to learn about very influential politicians from different countries, and belonging to different faiths, who manipulate the fate of humanity, and even very ordinary people, through an international organization headquartered in Europe?

I am willing to give you their names, and a detailed description of their political and economical agenda. Please believe me, that you see them almost every day on television, where they fight each other verbally, when competing for a public office or an election. But as soon as this public charade, or masquerade, is over, they go to their secret meetings to decide the fate of nations.

"I have to tell you something personal," he said gently. "I think you are ready for it. Twelve years ago, we met for the first time. We fell in love." This did not exactly surprise me, since I found him extremely attractive, but I was at a loss to understand why I did not remember our previous meeting, and asked him about it.

"You would have remembered, but you have asked me to wipe out the memory – for a while, at least. You see, you were a very young girl, not yet in college. We were together for a while, and you became pregnant – by the Anunnaki way, which is very different from human sexuality. You told me that you cannot as yet handle the burden, would rather, if possible, get on with your life, but you could not abandon the baby if you remembered him. I explained to you that this was, really, a very good decision. I had important plans for your son."

Well, the plans were astounding. Sinhar Marduchk had a family in mind, a wonderful couple that he wished would adopt our son, belonging to a very powerful Washington dynasty. He wanted our son to be raised as a politician, to learn the ropes, and eventually become an important member of government. The couple he had in mind was also descendants of the Anunnaki, decent, intelligent, and longing for a child.

To make a long story short, he manipulated their minds to believe that the woman had given birth to this infant, and rearranged the paperwork so that the birth certificate would say so. The lady actually came out of a hospital carrying the infant, accompanied by her proud husband, and the whole hospital crew also had their minds manipulated to believe the events. He took care to do the same with the couple's friends and relatives. Manipulating minds and events is something the Anunnaki can do very well.

"So where is the child now?" I asked Sinhar Marduchk.

"He is going to school in Washington, doing very well. Your son will grow up to be a credit to us."

Now I understood my life so much better. This must be why I never married, why I even disliked dating. Deep in my brain I knew I was married to this wonderful, spiritual, kind individual, and anyone else would never do.

I do not want to weary you with personal details, but of course Sinhar Marduchk and I acknowledged our married state. We could not live together on a regular basis, since he had to spend much of his time on his home planet, Aldebaran (Ashtari) and I could not stay there more than a few years at a time because my body would not withstand it without many changes. My husband promised me a very long life, and most important, that as the years go by I will develop the necessary physical attributes that would allow me to stay permanently on Ashtari.

We had a daughter, which is very different in her interests from my son, who is now a senator on earth. She is a linguist, and the number of languages she speaks is astounding. I am very proud of her.

I am now sixty years old, but of course age mean nothing to anyone who is married to an Anunnaki. I look considerably younger, and my husband, who knows so much, promises me that not only I shall live a very long life, but that death itself does not exist. When we die we move on to another dimension, giving up our physical bodies, and where we go is very much influenced by our thoughts and desires. As my husband promised me, I shall live until he is ready to move on, and then we can spend eternity together. So there is nothing to be afraid of, ever.

There is so much more to tell, but this letter is so long already, I am afraid you will put it aside and refuse to read more. I do hope I have given you something to think about, and perhaps, if you like, we can correspond. It is up to you – I will be happy to be the conduit through which the Anunnaki speaks with humanity.

Mr. de Lafayette, I know you are a very scientific person, and because you have practiced law, as I have found out, you want facts, not fiction. Don't ever believe or let your readers believe that communication with extraterrestrials can be done through channeling, as many people pretend.

This is impossible, because they are in different worlds and your thoughts and state of trance could not reach them through certain frequencies.

The human thoughts, even though they emanate frequencies and vibes like electrical and radio emissions, they do stop at the end of the solar system, and the mind transmission cannot go beyond that limit. Extraterrestrial have not and would not communicate telepathically. If you show interest in my letter, I will show you step by step, detail by detail, how communication can be done with an extraterrestrial, as my Anunnaki husband taught me. I can stay in constant contact with you to tell you where the Anunnaki descendants live, in what countries, in what cities, and how to recognize them. Also, I might mention that they do come not only from Ashtari, but from several other planets, as the United States government and scientists from Europe will discover before 2022."

141

Excerpts from her second letter: The following material is the second letter I received from her. Again, it is in her own words and I will not attempt to change, edit, or even form judgment.

"Dear Mr. de Lafayette:

Since you have so kindly shown an interest in my story, I am writing to you again, and this time I plan to give you much more elaborate information.

Therefore, I think it may be advisable to separate the material under explanatory titles. This way we will avoid confusion, and present the information in manageable sizes.

The first genetically created race could not speak, and the concept of language was completely unknown to them. Thousands of years later, the Anunnaki taught the newly race of humans how to speak, read, and write.

The Anunnaki's first genetically created human race was the seed of humanity as we know it; they were the ancestors of modern humans, beginning to populate the earth 25,000 years before the construction of the great pyramids.

I am only citing the pyramids as a landmark in human history to give you a chronological perspective.

Greater, taller and bigger monuments were erected centuries before the construction of the pyramids, and some ruins can still be found in Phoenicia (Modern Lebanon today) particularly in Baalbeck, and in Mesopotamia (Modern Iraq today).

Contrary to all beliefs, including what Judaism, Christianity and Islam teach us, Eve was not created from the rib of Adam. Men were created from an early female form that was "fertilized" by the leaders and the elite of the Anunnaki.

They lived in quarantine cities, and had both sons and daughters fathered by the Anunnaki.

Some of the most puzzling sites of these cities, due to their size and functionality, were in Ur, Amrit, Ugarit, Petra (Batra), Tyre and Sidon. Early humans who lived during that era called the quarantined city of these women "The City of Mirage", and "The City of Beautiful Illusion," since the most attractive women from earth lived there. And the quasi-humans who were made out of earth were *not* allowed to interact with these women.

Thousands of years later, the inhabitants of what is today the Arab Peninsula and the lands bordering Persia, the United Arab Emirates, and India, called these women "The Women of Light", and those who were allowed to "mix with them" were called "The Sons of Light".

From this early human race, all humans came to life. God had nothing to do with us. In other words, the God we know, revere, and fear today did not create us.

Even the word or term "God" did not exist in the early stages of the existence of the human race on earth.

Instead "Gods" or "Heavenly Masters" were used.

And thousands of years later, those terms were changed to "Giants," "Elohim," "Nephilim," "Anakim," "Fallen Angels," you name it...

Some 300,000 years before the creation of the cities of "The Women of Lights," forty-six different races of humans and quasi-humans populated the earth. The greatest numbers were found in Africa, Madagascar, Indonesia, Brazil, and Australia. These races died out not because of famine, ecological catastrophes, or acts of war, but because of the disintegration of the very molecules and composition of their cells. The Anunnaki created the "final form" of human beings, and we, all the ordinary and normal people are their descendants.

Eusebius, the Bishop of Cæsarea, Palestine, had genealogical records of the descendants of the Anunnaki who became Syriac. At the Council of Antioch in 363 A.D., Bishop Eusebius intended to bring this subject in his "Theophania" to the attention of the members of the Council. But for obvious reasons, no additional information or manuscripts about what happened at the Council were provided. In the Syriac manuscripts of Zachariah of Mitylene, who frequently corresponded with Eupraxius, two references were made to the Anunnaki as the ancestors of the Ashurian-Syriac. Another bishop by the name of Proterius tried to destroy these letters. Fortunately, two hand-written copies were made, as the tradition of this era dictated, and were saved in the vault of a scribe. Those letters resurfaced in 1957 in a personal acquisition of Cardinal Maouchi, the Patriarch of the Maronite Church in Lebanon. After of Maouchi's death, those files were kept in the secret vaults of Al-Kaslik Monastery in Lebanon.

The original language of the Anunnaki is still intact and is currently being used by top American scientists and researchers who work in secret American-Aliens military bases in the United States and Mexico.

In 1947, the first attempt was made by American linguists, who previously worked at the OSS (Precursor to the CIA), to decipher it. They tried to compare it with the Sumerian, Hebrew, Armenian and Phoenician Alphabet, languages which are directly derived from the Anunnaki's written language.

The problem they faced and could not resolve were the geometrical symbols included in the written Anunnaki's texts. But in 1956, they cracked down the puzzle.

Those mathematical figures hold great secrets regarding an alien advanced technology used for peaceful and constructive purposes. The American military intelligence and what's left from Dr. Fermi's group at Los Alamos wanted to use this alien technology for military purposes.

The earliest among the final terrestrial human race were the Phoenicians, the Hyksos, the Philistines, the very early Etruscans, the earliest Druids, Minoan, people of Mu, and the first inhabitants of Sumeria.

Later on, the Ashurians resided among the last remnants of the Anunnaki who visited earth and lived there for 600 more years. After that, the Anunnaki left earth for good, never to return again, except as visitors.

One of the reasons for their departure was the discovery of the "tree of life", also known as "The Tree of Knowledge" by humans – a metaphor for the acquisition of knowledge and understanding by the human race, on its own. The acquisition of this supreme knowledge caused the humans to rebel against the Anunnaki.

The Anunnaki have two kinds or styles of languages; one is spoken and the other one is written. The spoken language is the easiest one to learn, and it is used by the Anunnaki's population. The written one is exclusively used in books and consists of twenty-six letters. Seven of these letters represent the planets that surround their star. Many of the Anunnaki's letters cannot be pronounced by Westerners because of the limitation of their vocal chords. There are seven additional letters that are complete words, and these words represent the attributes of their "Grand Leader."

Translated into terrestrial language, the grand leader becomes the creator of energy, in other words, "God."

However, the Anunnaki do not believe in a God in the same sense we do, even though they were the ones who created and originated the early forms of religions on earth.

The god they brought to earth is a vengeful and terrifying god, something that the Gnostics and early scholars of the Coptic Church in Egypt were fully aware of. Their doctrines show their disdain for such a god, and consequently, they called him the "Creator of Evil and Darkness."

Later on in history, the early Gnostics began to spread the word that this earth was not created by the God of the Church, but rather by an evil demigod. The early human beings who interacted with the Anunnaki shared similar beliefs.

But they were mistaken, and were intentionally mislead by a lower class of the Anunnaki who hated other extraterrestrials who visited the earth, and particularly by the Igigi who treated humans like slaves and robotic machines.

Scholars like Sitchin and Gardner have equated the Anunnaki with the Nephilim. This is not totally correct. The lower class of the Anunnaki are the Nephilim, although many historians call them sometimes Anakim or Elohim. The higher class of the Anunnaki is ruled by Baalshalimroot, and his followers or subjects are called the "Shtaroout-Hxall Ain", meaning the inhabitants of the house of knowledge, or "those who see clearly."

The word "Ain" was later adopted by the early inhabitants of the Arab Peninsula. "Ain" in Arabic means "eye".

In the secret teachings of Sufism, visions of Al Hallaj, and of the greatest poetess of Sufism, Rabiha' Al Adawi Yah, known as "Ha Chi katou Al Houbb Al Ilahi" (The mistress of the divine love), and in the banned book *Shams Al Maa'Ref Al Kubrah* (Book of the Sun of the Great Knowledge), the word "eye" meant the ultimate knowledge, or wisdom from above. "Above" clearly indicates the heavens.

Later on, it was used to symbolize the justice of God or "God watching over us." And much later in history, several societies and cultures adopted the "eye" as an institutional symbol and caused it to appear on many temples' pillars, bank notes, money bills, and religious texts. The Freemasons' and Illuminati's favorite symbol is the Anunnaki's eye.

And as everything changes in life and takes on different forms and meanings, the "eye" became a "triangle," a very secretive and powerful symbol. George Washington carried this triangle with him wherever he went, and wore it during official ceremonies. If you double and reverse the triangle, you get the Star of David.

This very triangle is visible on many extraterrestrial spacecrafts and on uniforms of military personnel in secret American military bases underground, working on alien technology and propulsion systems.

The powerful Trilateral Commission was founded by David Rockefeller, the Chairman of the Chase Manhattan Bank of New York, in July 1973. It is recorded that in their first board meeting, Rockefeller proposed to adopt the Anunnaki's triangle as the official symbol/logo of this world organization.

According to an official statement issued by the Commission, the principal and official aim of the Trilateral Commission is "to harmonize the political, economic, social, and cultural relations between the three major economic regions in the world." The Commission divided the world into a triangle joining three regions consisting of the Far East, Europe, and North America, all within the perimeter of a triangle. Basically, the Trilateral Commission aims at controlling the world under the auspices of a centralized American power-group consisting of bankers, financiers, selected political leaders, top military echelon and members of the cabinet from each administration.

On February 17, 1953, an American millionaire by the name of Paul Warburg shouted before the Senate of the United States of America: "We shall have world government whether or not you like it, by conquest or consent."

Many members of the Trilateral Commission are descendants of a lower class of an extraterrestrial race. Some passed away, but many of them still live among us. It is impossible for ordinary people to recognize them. But the good and decent descendants of our extraterrestrial teachers can identify them very easily.

In future letters, I will give you their names and explain their plans.

When integrated without balance and cosmic harmony (spatial equilibrium) in architectural design and lining up territories, the triangle becomes a negative force on the map.

My husband told me that if the three sides of the triangle are separated, such separation can cause serious health problems. The triangle becomes three lines of negative energy.

This energy is not easily detected; nevertheless it runs strong and deep underground.

People who live above these lines suffer enormously. In many instances, this negative power or current can negatively affect the present and future of many human beings.

Similar to some Ufologists who can identify UFOs' hot spots on earth, usually above ground; descendants of the extraterrestrials can identify and locate the negative currents underground. Each country has these negative currents or circuits underground. I do not wish to scare you, but I must inform you that some American states are located above these lines; for example, Mississippi, Alabama, the northern part of Washington, DC, and two areas in Brooklyn, New York share this misfortune.

Many of the Phoenician linguists and early creators of their Alphabet borrowed numerous words and expressions from the higher class of the Anunnaki.

Ancient Phoenician texts and poems, recorded on tablets found in Tyre and Sidon, included reference to symbols and words taken from the written language of the upper class of the Anunnaki. Members of an early Anunnaki expedition to Phoenicia taught the Phoenicians how to create their language, and revealed to them the secret powerful names and attributes of Baalshalimroot.

They instructed them not to use these words for ill purposes. Particularly, the word "Baalazamhour-Il" is never to be said, spelled, or written.

Later on in history, the Hebrews religiously observed this instruction, and pronouncing the word of name of God became forbidden. However, the Anunnaki revealed to the Phoenicians and Sumerians seven positive and powerful names/attributes of the Grand Leader.

If well used, these words can bring prosperity, good health, and salvation in moments of difficulty.

147

The prophet Mohammad learned these seven words from an early Christian ascetic, a Sahara hermit called Raheb Bouhayra. Today, Muslims all over the world are aware of these seven words or names. They call them in written Arabic "Asma' Al Lah Al Sabha' Al Housna," meaning the seven lovely names of God.

Those names do not have numerical value or secret meanings as many scholars claim, simply because they were not originally written in a geometrical form. None of these words appeared in the so-called hieroglyphic measuring tape that the Americans found at the crash site in Roswell. The symbols and geometrical signs Americans found in Roswell were biochemical symbols.

The American top military scientists who work in secret military bases and aliens' laboratories on earth have an extraterrestrial lexicon, and use it constantly. In that lexicon, or dictionary, you will find variations of Phoenician and Sumerian symbols.

Some letters represent maritime and celestial symbols and measurements. The fact that the Americans are still using this extraterrestrial language should be enough to convince you that extraterrestrials, Anunnaki and Ashtari (Aldebaran) descendants, live among us, otherwise why would anyone learn a language that cannot used to communicate with people who speak it and write it?

On some of the manifestos of military parts used in anti-gravity secret laboratories underground in the United States, several letters were borrowed from the "Enuma Elish" of Sumeria and regularly appeared on the top right corner of each document. In the eighties, those Sumerian numbers were replaced by an Americanized version.

It is true that the Sumerian ancient texts and records mentioned names of some of the Anunnaki leaders such as Utu, Ningishzida, Ninki, Marduk, Enki, Enlil, Inanna, but the greatest name of all remains Baalshalimroot, also referred to as "Baalshalimroot-An'kgh." Terah, the father of Abraham, mistakenly worshiped Baalshalimroot-An'kgh. Early Semites made the same mistake when they worshiped the leaders of the Anunnaki as gods who later became Bene Ha-Elohim, meaning the children of gods. The Anunnaki never introduced themselves as gods.

148

The words: El Elyon and Yahweh or Jehovah were taken directly from the Anunnaki's written language. The original word was "Yah'weh-El' Ankh" and El Elyon was "Il Ilayon-imroot."
The Early Anunnaki who visited earth were extremely tall. Some reached the height of 9 feet, and lived as long as 400,000 years. These Anunnaki did not leave descendants on earth.
Those who came to earth much later, before the regional deluge, and right after that huge Tsunami, left families behind them when they returned home.

By home, I mean Zeta Reticuli and Ashartartun-ra. These families are the origin of the hybrids and/or extraterrestrial human beings living today among us. It is very important to learn and remember this.
Mr. de Lafayette, even though I have given you quite a bit of scientific and historical data, I don't want you to think that this is all I have to say. My relationship with the Anunnaki is personal, loving, and involving family and friends.
We must seek similarities and affiliations between sentient beings, rather than always harp on the differences. I want to tell you so much more – I want the world to know about my dear sister-in-law, Sinhar Marduchk's twin sister, who came all the way to earth to help me choose a dress for my wedding, and became my closest friend. I want to tell you all about the guests who came to our wedding – and what a list that was...I want you to know about my nieces and nephews and the other lovely Anunnaki children I met on my own trips to Ashtari.
We had hours of fun as the children demonstrated their shape-changing talents to me, assuming what they thought would be such frightening or amusing personalities.
So I would like to hope that this is the beginning of a profitable and pleasant correspondence, even friendship, even though we can never meet in person.
All the best..."

And here is the story and material I received from her (Excerpts):
My first meeting with the extraterrestrials, and the bizarre plan they made me follow.
February 1965, Maine: At this time of year darkness fell early, and the roads were not busy on that extremely cold night.

149

I was enjoying the drive despite the snowy and slippery conditions because I was so young, and just having a car was a novelty and an adventure. I was going home after an afternoon's study at a good friend's house. We planned to prepare for our high school finals, but we were so excited about the prospect of college, that we could barely concentrate.

Both of us applied to the archaeology-anthropology department of a well-known New York university, and were thrilled with the fact that our parents would allow us to spend four years on our own in the huge and exciting city.

As I cautiously wound my way, I was dreaming about myself in New York, wearing sophisticated clothes and drinking coffee at some marvelous little places, when I noticed that a large vehicle, possibly a lorry, was blocking the road at a little distance. I could not make it out clearly, so I drove carefully until I was about fifteen feet or so behind it. I was considering going to the vehicle to see if the driver needed help, when I suddenly noticed a bright, yellow shaft of light moving from the vehicle toward me. It was a dusty sort of light, with particles moving in it at a random motion, much like a sunbeam through a window on a summer afternoon, but brighter and highly visible against the dark evening. I stared at the light, trying to figure out what it could possibly be, until it stopped just in front of my car.

The little particles stopped moving in their crazy random way, and instead, started to coagulate, moving toward the center in a rather orderly way. I was mesmerized by the movement, and I cannot tell how long it took, but I think only a few minutes. The particles at the center formed a globe, while the rest of the shaft of light was clean and empty of particles.

Then, a sudden visual but silent explosion took place in the center – there is really no other way to describe the phenomenon – as if the center burst into fireworks. Then, the fireworks rearranged themselves into the shape of a baby!

Suddenly I was horribly afraid. Before I saw the baby form, it could have been a natural phenomenon of some sort, but when this shape took place, no reasonable explanation existed. I looked at it, not knowing what to do and feeling trapped, since I could not drive away and escape with the vehicle in front of me on the narrow road, nor could I turn the car.

Leaving the car and running would be insane. I sat, trembling, and the baby form started growing. It expanded, changed, filled out the shaft, and seemed to become a grown-up man.

But the man was deformed. Part of his back overlapped his neck, his hips jutted away from his body, and the face was blurred. My heart was beating so quickly that I felt it would explode, too.

The fear almost paralyzed me, and then everything became even worse. The man rearranged himself and became normal, and stepped out of the shaft of light. The shaft remained where it was, waving gently and illuminating the man.

He waved at me, in a friendly and normal fashion, and moved toward my car, but I still could not see his face since the light was behind him. All I saw was something really horrifying. The man's eyes were glowing in the relative darkness, like the eyes of a wolf. Like two little lantern, they shown at me as he approached.

I think I screamed, because the man, suddenly realizing my terror, waved his hand in a circular motion, the shaft of light moved to his side, illuminating the most handsome face I had ever seen.

The striking face was matched by the rest of his physique. I am tall, five feet eleven inches in my bare feet, but this man seemed to be almost seven feet tall, like some of the basketball players I used to watch. And the broad shoulders and perfect proportions, clearly visible in the uncanny illumination, added to his movie-star attraction. He seemed to be in his mid twenties.

The glow in his eyes subsided, but the eyes in that perfect face were still not normal. They seemed to glitter, so brightly that I was not able to make out their color. I could not take my own eyes off them, as if hypnotized, and was not able to move at all; my limbs felt as if they were made of iron.

I have no idea if my paralysis happened because of the fear, or because it does occur every so often when humans meet aliens, though not in every case. Then the glitter died down, and I could see that his eyes were very dark, almost black in the golden light, and very large, much like my own. As a matter of fact, the man's olive skin and black hair were exactly like mine. My paralysis completely disappeared.

"I hope I have not frightened you," he said. Kind words, but I did not even notice that he knew my name, because his voice was so startling. It sounded like one of those old records you played on an old-fashioned turntable – if you put it on the wrong speed, it became fast, squeaky, and scratchy, very unpleasant. He stopped, made some elaborate movements with his hands, and spoke again, this time with a very pleasant, normal human voice. "I am sorry. I am a bit out of practice, and these changes and adaptations of my traveling form into regular shape and sound can be tricky."
I found my voice.
"Regular shape and sound?
Who are you?
What are you?
And what do you want of me?
Yes, you scared me a lot – I should think you could have changed before I came and then stopped me in a simpler way, rather than do this dramatic appearance, like a grade B horror movie?" I was infuriated, but astonishingly, no longer terrified.

At the time, I could not understand why I was not paralyzed with terror. Now, of course, I know that part of my mind was willing to accept it, which makes sense in the light of the events that followed, and the secrets that were told. But also, let's face it, perhaps I was also influenced by the mysterious stranger's great looks... teenage girls *can* be silly about very handsome men.
The stranger laughed at my defiant words, but rather kindly, not at all in a mocking way.
Later, he confessed that he was quite relieved that I was exasperated rather than horrified to a point of fainting or shrieking helplessly. "You are right. I should have thought about a nicer way to meet you. I apologize...Anyway, to answer your very reasonable questions, my name is Sinhar Marduchk and I am an Anunnaki."
"Well, I am pleased to meet you, Mr. Sin... Mard... Sorry, I can't say your name too well."
"No wonder. It's quite a name, I suspect. But some of my human friends call me Marduchk at first," said the apparition, his teeth gleaming by the light of the shaft. "Eventually, they get used to the long name."

"My name is Victoria... wait, you just called me by my name. I was too confused to notice. You know me?"

"Of course I know you. I came specifically to meet you. We have a small job for you to do, if you agree to cooperate with us."

"What sort of job?" I asked suspiciously.

"I wonder if I can tell you without some preparation," he said. "It has something to do with who you really are."

"I see," I said. "So you know I am adopted. You know a lot about me, Marduchk. It's a little disconcerting."

"I know more than you think, to be honest, but no, you should not worry about it. Naturally, when you want someone to perform a very important task, you try to learn something about them, right?" said Marduchk.

"And yes, of course I know you were adopted. That is the whole point."

Indeed, I was adopted in infancy by a wonderful couple who made excellent parents, and loved me very much. I would have known I was adopted even if they had not told me, because I had olive skin, black hair, and eyes that were so dark as to be almost black, as I mentioned before.

My parents, whose ancestors came from England, were both blond. A couple of years ago I expressed a wish to find who were my birth parents, and my adoptive parents tried their very best to help, but we did not have any luck. Wherever we turned, all the information was blocked, deleted, or carefully hidden away.

We finally gave up, and I was not too troubled about it after all. I had such a good life at home, I knew I did my best to find out the truth, and not succeeding, I decided to just forget about the whole issue and get on with my life. I must say my parents were much relieved, they were afraid I would mope about it.

"So do tell," I said.

"You were born in Lebanon," said Marduchk. "Your birth parents were Ashurians, who are Middle Eastern Christians, related to the Syriacs, who still speak Aramaic among themselves."

"Wow, Lebanon, of all places. No wonder we could not fine out anything about my birth parents, it's a different country, even a different continent..." I said.

"I have something to tell you about them, too," he said. "The reason why I was sent to meet you was that your DNA, which of course you inherited from both of your birth parents, is very rich in Anunnaki genes. All modern humans have Anunnaki genes, since the original human race, as you know it, was the product of the Anunnaki and what was the human race in ancient times, but some people, in certain areas of the world, maintained a stronger pool.
Many live in Iraq, of course, since it exists on top of the Sumerian and Babylonian civilizations."
"I am an Anunnaki? Like you, then?" I have to admit that while this may be shocking to some, to me it sounded like a wonderful fairy tale. Besides, having common ground with this gorgeous guy was not so bad...
"Well, yes, you are, to a large extent. Not totally an Anunnaki, and physically changed by your life on earth, but close enough."
"And you chose me specifically for some splendid job?"
"I don't know if you will find it splendid. Well, maybe you will, since it involves some courage and some sacrifice."
"Maybe you want me to be a spy? Or an agent?
Hunt bad aliens that fight good aliens like you? Will I be carrying a space weapon?"
"Nothing like it. Sorry. It's totally different."
"Am I the first one to be chosen?"
"Oh, no. We have to employ many people.
We always contact many women, since women are paramount in our experiments, much more important than men, I am afraid.
But you were personally selected for this particular task, that is, if you agree to do it." I rather liked hearing how important women were in the Anunnaki's plans. Usually, I felt women had to always fight for their rights.
"Why are you employing humans, anyway?
What are the connections between the Anunnaki and us?"
"We are your creators. The Anunnaki's first genetically created human race was the seed of humanity as you know it, the ancestors of modern humans, beginning to populate the earth 25,000 years before the construction of the great pyramids.
Contrary to all of your social and religious beliefs, including what Judaism, Christianity and Islam teach you, Eve was not created from the rib of Adam.

Men were created from an early female form that was 'fertilized' by the leaders and the elite of the Anunnaki. The women lived in quarantined cities, and had both sons and daughters fathered by the Anunnaki.

Thousands of years later, the inhabitants of what is today the Arab Peninsula and the lands bordering Persia, the United Arab Emirates, and India, called these women 'The Women of Light', and those men who were allowed to mix with them, including their sons, were called 'The Sons of Light.' From this early human race, all humans came to life."

"What about God and his creation?" I asked.

"God had nothing to do with us," said Marduchk. "In other words, the God you know, revere, and fear today did not create you. Even the word or term 'God' did not exist in the early stages of the existence of the human race on earth. Instead 'Gods' or 'Heavenly Masters' were used. And thousands of years later, those terms were changed to 'Giants,' 'Elohim,' 'Nephilim,' 'Anakim,' 'Fallen Angels,' you name it..."

"So the Bible was not entirely right," I said, reflecting on my Sunday School lessons.

"Some is right, some is myth, some is fable," said Marduchk. "But it has great stories. I personally like it very much."

"This is fantastic," I said. "Scary, though."

"As a matter of fact, it should not be scary. Some day I will tell you how much there is nothing to fear, how much we are all the children of the universe and of eternity, and how we can look forward to eons of joy and peace. But we can't go into it now. We must concentrate on our task."

"So you still take an interest in our affairs?"

"Yes, even though at some point you rebelled against us... but then again, don't all children rebel against their parents, and the parents still love them? We do love you..."

"What do I have to do?" I was not going to refuse, even though I was a bit scared of what was to come. I knew that if I refused, he would go away and contact another girl, and I did not want to lose him. I was already beginning to fall in love, even though of course I did not know it.

"Have a baby," he said simply.

"WHAT?" I screamed. "I am not yet eighteen years old! I can't get married and have babies! I am going to college next year!"

"You don't have to get married. You don't have to raise the baby. We have plans for this baby. We just want your genetic material, always with your permission."

"Plans? For my baby? Doesn't a baby need a mother? Are you people as cruel and as mad as to deprive a child of his mother?"

"This baby has to grow to be a pivotal figure in the government of this country. He is important for world peace, for recovery from hunger and want, for freedom. He has a great task ahead of him, which I can already tell you he will fulfil admirably, since I am able to see a great deal of the future, though not all, not the part which requires free will.

Therefore, we have a couple in mind who will adopt this child. Both belong to very powerful Washington dynasties, they are longing for a child, and they are decent and intelligent. They will be extremely kind and loving to their child. What's more, I am going to manipulate their minds.

They will believe that the baby is their birth child, that the woman has actually given birth to this child. I will change all the records, rearrange the paperwork and the birth certificate, and at the right moment the woman will come out of the hospital, carrying the infant and accompanied by her proud husband.

The whole hospital crew will have their minds manipulated to believe all these events."

I was quiet, thinking. Marduchk was quiet, letting me mull over it. Finally I said, "My goodness, the things you can do... Anyway, if I agree, I have a condition."

"Which is?"

"You said you can manipulate minds. If I agree, I want you to make me forget the whole incident, until I am ready to face the situation. I cannot bring myself knowingly, consciously, to give away my baby; I simply cannot perform such an act. But I can see that it is needed, and in addition, for some reason I simply can't bring myself to refuse. Can you do that?"

"It will be very easy," said Marduchk. "And I can revive your memory when you have accomplished everything you want to do, and we can meet again and take up our lives from there.

156

We can even decide at what age you would want to do it. Would you feel more comfortable if we got married first?"

"You want to marry me?" I felt elated, in my teenage way, but thoroughly confused.

"Yes, I do," said Marduchk in the most matter of fact way. "I am, after all, going to be in charge of this baby. And I know we will be very happy together, if you accept."

He was going to be involved with my baby. One way or another, Marduchk was to remain a permanent factor in my life, if I accept. If I don't accept, Marduchk will disappear from my life, and make me forget this has ever happened. Why did he matter so much to me? And why did I trust him so implicitly? He was almost a hallucination, and yet I did trust him, completely. But marriage? That was the issue.

"No," I said decisively. "I am too young to marry. When we meet again, if we feel we want to do that, then we shall. I suspect I will want to marry you very much, but let's wait on that. However, I will take up the task. I accept it."

"That is wonderful," said Marduchk.

"As for the marriage, I promise you I will not change my mind; an Anunnaki never does. And you will know your own mind then."

"But how can I disappear for the nine months of pregnancy? I can't let my parents know, they will be horrified."

"You don't have to," said Marduchk. "For us, past, present, and future are all one and the same.

I will take you away on my machine to where you shall spend the time quite happily with my sister and me, and when I have the baby safely in my arms, and you are well and on your feet, I will return you to this car, one second after our current conversation. You will know nothing, forget it ever happened, drive home safely, and get on with your life. And ten, twelve years from now, you will have a little surprise. We will then see how good I was in my brain manipulation..."

"I hope I really do forget," I said. "If I have bits and pieces of memory intruding on me it would be so confusing. And yet, I have to give everything up for so long. This is all so confusing."

"I have an idea that might cheer you up," said Marduchk. "How would you like to speak your own language, Aramaic?"

His smiling, large, black Anunnaki eyes were full of humor.

"Of course, I would love to, it would be wonderful," I said. "But it probably will take years to learn, right?"

"Wrong," said Marduchk. He looked into my eyes and his own eyes started acting as before, with the hypnotic glittering light. I felt paralyzed again, but only for a few seconds. Then it stopped, I shook myself, and to my utter disbelief found myself speaking and understanding a language that I have never heard before.

"Will I forget it as soon as we part?" I asked, enjoying speaking in Aramaic.

"No, it is my gift to you. You can now read and write it, too. It will be great for your college studies, considering the subject you have chosen.

You will believe, and tell your teachers, that you have learned it on your own when you were in high school, in preparation for your archaeology and history college career, from various books.

These books are now on your shelf, at home, I just placed them there. They look well used, and your parents are going to believe it, too."

By now, I was not even surprised that Marduchk knew what subject I was about to major in. Incidentally, Marduchk and I always speak to each other in Aramaic, and such a pleasure it is to be able to share something that is so close to our emotional core.

"Very well, let's get on with it" I said, rather bravely getting out of the car. We walked toward his vehicle. I must admit I felt very important... again, girls can be so silly sometimes. I did not really grasp then that so many women have been approached, over the centuries, for such important tasks; significant motherhood is a universal pattern. Still, looking back, I am so happy I followed my instincts, trusted Marduchk, and helped shape humanity in my own little way. And how rewarding it turned out for my own life as well, I can't even begin to tell.

April 1977, New York: I took the subway from fifty-third street to my home in Greenwich Village. Dinner with Marge was pleasant, she is a good friend, but why do women always have to concentrate on what is wrong? Why do we complain so much to each other? Life has been pretty good until this point, after all.

When I graduated from college, I decided not to continue with a graduate program, for two reasons.

First, I always felt that the classes lacked something, that history, anthropology, and archaeology missed something very important and was always inaccurate. Second, I was not sure I was the right fit for academia.

So I took a job in retail, since New York had so many of these positions in the myriad clothing and accessories lines, and I love fashion. I did well and was quickly advancing in my position, when tragedy struck.

In 1973, my parents were killed in an automobile accident, hit by a drunk driver, who was killed as well. I was lost for a while, sunk into depression and felt I was all alone in the world.

However, after a few months I decided to pull myself together since I knew my parents would not have wanted me to destroy myself by protracted mourning.

I looked into my financial situation, realized that the money they left me could help toward buying my own business, and bought a small store that sold accessories and costume jewelry.

I suppose I am a natural business woman, because even though I was so young, the store, which was failing with the previous owners, recovered and began to do very well.

As for Marge, she was an opera singer. She sang at the Met, and while not the star that she would have wanted to be, she was quite successful and always employed. But her personal life is sad. Marge longed to be married and have a family, and as we sat at dinner, she told me about all the men she had dated in the past year, all of them turning out to be no good.

"Maybe that is why I don't date at all," I said.

"I don't know how you can stand it," said Marge. "Don't you even want to try to marry, have a family?"

"I don't know, Marge," I said. "I have tried a few times. No one was good enough, I was bored to death with every one of them, so ordinary..."

"But what about sex?" she asked. "Don't you miss it?"

"I think sex is overrated," I said. We both laughed, but perhaps this is true for me; I was not particularly interested in sex. At any rate, I really never loved anyone, and I did not think this would change; I accepted that and did not seek a change. And yet I went home feeling slightly sad. I showered, went to bed, and started reading a new detective book by P.D. James.

I like her style and her understanding of true evil; I think she has a better grasp of human psychology than most professional therapists. Sad to say, though, I fell asleep just as the murderer was about to be caught.

Suddenly I woke up.

It was almost pitch black, since I prefer sleeping in the dark and never keep a nightlight. I usually sleep well and do not wake up at night, and if I do, I go right back to sleep. This time, after the large dinner Marge and I ate, I was very thirsty, and decided to go to the kitchen for a glass of water. I tried to turn on the lamp beside me, and to my amazement it just wasn't there. I thought I might have upset it somehow during the night, so I just stayed there for a few minutes to allow my eyes to adjust to the dark before getting up. Something was wrong. As I was beginning to make out the shapes of the furniture, it was clear to me that I did not wake up in my own apartment. Was I in a hospital?

Perhaps I had an accident.

Often, people who have a serious accident do not remember it right away. I tried to move, to see if I was hurt, and I felt just fine. So what in the world happened?

I sat on the bed, trying to decide what to do, and a dim light turned itself on.

I saw I was in a small bedroom, simply but nicely furnished, and certainly not in a hospital. "Please do not be alarmed, Victoria," said a very calm and pleasant female voice through an intercom.

Ah, the nurse, I thought, still clinging to my idea of a mishap. Perhaps I had a stroke? I was a bit too young for that at age thirty, but one never knows, things like that do happen, and after all, I had no idea of my birth parents' medical history.

"Where am I?" I asked. "Am I ill? Or hurt?"

"Not at all," said the voice. "You are quite well, you just happen to be our guest. I will be with you in a few moments. There is a robe hanging on the chair, and a glass of water on the little table next to your bed. The bathroom is behind the door on the right side of your bed. Would you like me to bring you a cup of tea, or perhaps coffee?"

"Coffee will be wonderful," I said, my alarm subsiding. This was mysterious, but I was sure the nurse, or attendant, or whoever she was, would explain.

160

I put on the robe, drank my water, went to the bathroom to wash my face and see if my hair needed fixing, and then sat waiting for the nurse to come. A light knock on the door, and a most attractive woman came in, carrying a tray.

She wore a black outfit, which immediately settled that she was not a nurse. She was tall and elegant. Her eyes were large and black, much like mine, and her hair, which was also black and softly curly, had a beautiful reddish sheen, making it glow under the dim lights.

"I am so happy to make your acquaintance, Victoria," she said. "My name is Miriam. At least, this is the closest I can get to my real name, which is Sinhar Semiramicsh, which I imagine would be a little difficult for you to pronounce, at present." She poured out a cup of coffee for me. "Milk and sugar?" she asked.

"Just milk, please," I said. "What an interesting name. I can't make out from where it comes. Where were you from?"

"It is an Anunnaki name," said Miriam casually. "You may have heard of us before." She looked at me in a curious way, as if she expected something from me, but I could not imagine what it was, and so I sipped my excellent coffee. "I have heard the name Anunnaki, many years before, in school," I said. "I recall they are a vanished race that have lived in the Middle East, but obviously I am wrong, since you are an Anunnaki. Or do you just bear an ancient name, and the people did vanish?"

"No, we have not vanished," said Miriam. "Western archaeology and history do make some mistakes."

"Tell me about it," I said somewhat bitterly. "That is what made me leave the field, in which I majored; nothing was taught right, or so I thought at the time. So where are the Anunnaki to be found these days?"

"There are many of them in Iraq," said Miriam. That did not ring a bell at all. "My brother will be here in a minute," she continued. "You have met him before. I wonder if you will remember him." Another knock on the door and a man walked in, looking vaguely familiar.

He was tall and unusually handsome, and greatly resembled his sister. In a flash of thought I felt it was strange that I could have forgotten having met such an amazing, arresting face, but he shook my hand in a friendly manner, and said "Semiramicsh, I think our guest is entitled to some explanations."

161

"Indeed, I would like to know where I am. I imagine something happened to me and you have rescued me? But what? I strongly remember having gone to sleep after having dinner with my friend Marge. All the details, even the conversation we had, are clear in my head."

"I think I will go back to my post and let you do the explanation, Sinhar Marduchk," said Miriam. "I shall see you soon, Victoria."

Sinhar Marduchk.

I knew I have heard this name before. Something in my brain shifted, moved, trembled, as if shaken by a sudden memory. This was a bizarre sensation I have never felt before. The man smiled. "It is beginning to work," he said. "I am returning your memory of our first meeting, and everything that followed. I have started when you were asleep."

I stared at him, suddenly alarmed. Maybe all this was not as benign as I thought? Maybe these two people, beautiful and charming as they seemed, actually kidnapped me?

Perhaps they had the most horrible plans for me? Where the hell was I? Sinhar Marduchk must have noticed my sudden change of mood, because he said, "I am sorry. I seem to have a knack of alarming you, for some reason...just like I have done the time we met. I must lack judgement, and perhaps I should have let Sinhar Semiramicsh do all that, but I was so anxious to see you again. Anyway, you are not kidnapped, you are not a prisoner. You can leave any time you wish; you are merely a guest. But I do beg you, stay just where you are for a few more minutes. You will know everything as soon as the memory takes effect." Like I had a choice, I thought bitterly. I have no idea where I am, where to go, what's going on. "Where am I?" I said. "Do tell me right now, I am getting very nervous."

"You are on our machine, our vehicle," he said. "We are traveling around while we talk to you, and my sister is minding it."

"So I can't get out even if I wanted to," I said, angrily. "Suppose I asked you to stop and let me out? Would you do that?" I tried to sound strong, but I lacked conviction. That something that was working in my brain was growing stronger, and I felt dizzy and confused. I could not have gone anywhere on my own. I could not even get up.

"Yes, I would let you go," said Sinhar Marduchk. "Of course I would, but I would have to watch over you while you walk, since right now you must be dizzy." He might have given me a drug, I thought dizzily. Oh my God, he is drugging me... what are they going to do to me... I felt very faint, the room was spinning around me. Suddenly it all stopped. I opened my eyes and screamed, "Marduchk! It's you!" and I fainted.

When I came to, I remembered everything. Marduchk was sitting right next to my bed, holding my hand, a very concerned look on his face.

Yes, I remembered everything...not only our first meeting, twelve years ago on the deserted road in Maine, but our time on Ashtari. "How is he?" I asked anxiously. "How is my baby?"

"He is very well," said Marduchk. "He has a wonderful family, his parents had two more boys, in the normal way, and he is the best big brother imaginable. He is doing extremely well in school, has lots of friends, and already told his parents that he is determined to go into politics when he grows up...they were not surprised, exactly, since they let him see and learn a lot about what is going on in Washington, and they do have all the necessary resources. What a nice couple. I got to know them well over the years. They love their children dearly. Would you like to see him?"

"Why yes, of course," I said, trembling. I have not seen my son since I let him go, all these years ago, and at the time could not stop crying until Marduchk did as he promised and took away the memory, returning me to my car, one second after our trip to Ashtari. I had no memory left at all.

I drove straight home, not even recalling why I stopped in the first place, and resumed my life.

Marduchk took out a small object from his pocket, looking like an ordinary flashlight. He touched something on it and a circle of light, about the size of a basketball, was created on the wall.

It stretched into a square, looking like a television screen, and something like a movie began to enfold.

I saw a little boy in a beautiful, sunny garden, stretched on the grass and reading a very large book for someone his age. His hair was black and what I could see from his face was very beautiful. Then two smaller boys came running to him, obviously calling him to do something, and he got up, smiling, and ran away with them, carrying his book. All three looked healthy and happy.

I felt good, though I realized I was crying. My baby was okay, and that was the most important thing. I smiled at Marduchk, and he turned the device off.

"What is his name?" I asked.

"Joseph," he said. "He will have quite a life, Victoria. And so will you. Don't be unhappy."

"I am not unhappy. At this time I can handle it, like I thought I would," I said. "I can live with the results of my actions, really I can, Marduchk. Don't be distressed for me."

"Do you remember your first day on Nibiru?" he asked, smiling.

"Oh, yes. How strange it was, landing and not being able to see anything, neither plants, nor buildings, nor people, with this heavy, strange atmosphere that would block my vision. And I was so afraid when you told me I can only see everything if I take the cure that would make my eyes adjust..."

"But you were brave enough to try, Victoria. And wasn't Ashtari beautiful?"

"I loved it. What a happy time it was with you and Semiramicsh. I learned so much and had such fun."

"And now you can come back to us."

"But I cannot live there, Marduchk. You know that. Not until many years pass and with the Anunnaki help, my body will grow and adjust to the Ashtari's conditions."

"What of it? You will live for hundreds of years, there is all the time in the world. Do you remember that part of your learning? You will live for centuries, and then we will pass together into eternity.

"I still don't quite understand eternity, I confess," I said.

"Eternity is not an easy concept," said Marduchk. "But you will, I promise you. There is no such thing as death, life is eternal. The Anunnaki know that, scientifically, not on faith alone, like you do on earth."

"How joyful to really know that you will never have to lose your loved ones," I said.

"And as time goes by, I will come to Earth often, and work with you on what is needed, and so will Sinhar Semiramicsh. And you will come to Ashtari for longer and longer periods. And you must remember what you have learned there – that you will never have to age, you can choose the physical age you wish to be at any time, and you can devote your time to anything you like to do."

"Do you remember, you taught me how to navigate time and space, at least the rudimentary principles? I would like to work on that, and then study historical periods by going there. Of course I will keep the store, the world must think I am leading a normal life on earth and making a living, but I could have such fun going to these places and times."

"Of course, and we will develop your gifts and abilities much further. Besides, we will enhance your language skills. Remember how you learned Aramaic instantly? We can have you develop this talent so you can learn any language, past or present, in the same way."

"This will help my studies tremendously, Marduchk. But we will always speak our own language, Aramaic, between us, won't we?"

"For ever and ever," said Marduchk. "It's still my favorite language. And you will love speaking Anunnaki, too."

At that moment, a knock was heard on the door, and Sinhar Semiramicsh came in. "So, Victoria, should we prepare for the wedding, Anunnaki style?" she asked, smiling. "Many friends are waiting for us on Ashtari. You should see the wedding dresses I got for you to choose from..." I had to laugh.

My first months on Ashtari:
My trip on the spaceship, my difficulties of adjusting to Ashtari, and the lifestyle of the Anunnaki on their home planet.

February 1965, Maine: Marduchk and I approached the spaceship. In the dim light, it looked seamless, rounded, and silvery, as if made from aluminum or stainless steel, though of course it could have been any other metal, as far as I knew.

A door glided silently and we entered a room.

At the time, I was not aware of the distinct levels that contained the scientific apparatus and the machinery that was used to guide the craft.

I was not thinking about such matters, anyway, being too absorbed with my own concerns, and with the fact that I was actually boarding a space ship, like something out of a science fiction movie.

I had an insane desire to say "Take me to your leader," but thankfully I avoided the bad joke and tried to not be stupidly hysterical.

Marduchk settled me in a small room on the middle level, attached to the control room and used for sitting when the craft was on automatic. It was stark, containing only a small table and few simple but comfortable chairs, all made of metal.

Everything was surrounded by a kind of archways that met in the center.

Marduchk went into the control room to activate the spaceship, and while he was away, the archways became transparent, and showed some writing in a language I could not understand. Then, he returned to the little room and sat down.

"I put the ship on an automatic," he said. "It won't be a long trip, we are using all the tricks of the trade, that is, in time and space. In the meantime, would you like a cup of normal, ordinary earth coffee?"

"Don't you drink some exotic and strange things that would probably kill me?"

"Yes, sometimes, but to tell you the truth, after my numerous trips to earth and many stays there, I became rather fond of coffee and I make a very good cappuccino. We poor travelers have to adapt..."

I laughed and accepted the offer. Marduchk stood up, waved his hands above the little table, and two big white cups of cappuccino, complete with perfect foam, appeared out of thin air.

"No, it's not magic," he said when my mouth dropped without any class or style.

"Merely a form of technology; I called some vibrations in. Would you like some sugar?"

He produced a beautiful cut crystal bowl. I said nothing, put some sugar in my cup, and sipped the cappuccino. It was superb, and the warmth of the cup helped me relax as I watched Marduchk bring, out of thin air, a bunch of really nice cookies and paper napkins. I nibbled on one of the cookies, my fear and nervousness returning.

A baby, I was thinking. What did I get myself into. I am too young, I don't want any man to touch me, not even this glorious specimen who can produce cookies from nothing. I am just not ready. My heroic and patriotic decision gave way to sheer terror, and my eyes filled with tears I could not control. For heaven's sake, I thought. I am alone in a spaceship with an alien being, going God knows where... have I gone mad?

166

Why didn't I run away into the woods?"

My fears must have shown very clearly, because Marduchk said, "I think it would be fair to tell you what you will have to do right now, rather than wait for the briefing on Ashtari.

I can see you are getting very nervous even though you are very bravely trying to hide it. Listen to me and stop being so scared. It is not at all ominous, Victoria. I promise you."

"Not ominous?" I burst out loud. "Even if we don't think of the baby quite as yet, I am supposed to mate with a total stranger – whoever he is – and even if it turns out to be you who would father the child, you are still a stranger. I am calling it mating because it is not love making when you don't know each other and only do it for procreation, like cattle! And you say it is not ominous?"

"You will not need to mate with anyone," said Marduchk calmly. "We could never ask a child like you to face such a frightening thing. No, in Ashtari we have our babies very differently."

"Whatever do you mean?" I asked, bewildered.

"How do I get pregnant if I don't have intercourse?"

"The Anunnaki have long ago separated love from procreation. We do marry, and we marry strictly for love.

Our unions are permanent. Once we make our choice for a life partner, we have no wish to stray and remain paired forever, like some birds do in your world. Certainly nothing like the marriage of humans, of which fifty percent end in divorce, or worse."

"So you don't have sex at all?"

"Not the way you do. Our way of expressing love is through light. When Union, as we call it, occurs, each partner starts to emit golden light. The lights grow strong, mingle, and this mingling causes intense physical, mental, and spiritual joy.

It is much better than anything humans experience though sex, since the sensations go directly to the brain. It is also much more beautiful, aesthetically, than any physical sex could be. What humans do, to put it plainly, may be pleasurable, but certainly not aesthetically pleasing..."

"Wow, that sounds nice, mingling lights, "I said. "Not at all frightening. I would actually like to try it."

For once, Marduchk seemed extremely startled at my blunt statement, and looked at me in a rather horrified way.

But then suddenly he laughed. "How human of you to say that," he said.

167

"You don't understand how serious the blending of lights is for an Anunnaki. It's sacred, really. You don't just try it with anyone, ever. You must be married first."

I felt a little subdued, as if I said something terribly inappropriate. "So what will happen to me?" I said.

"You will go into a very nice hospital-like place," said Marduchk, obviously relieved to get away from the previous subject that seemed to embarrass him. "They will help you lie down on a table, much like one of the examination tables in any doctor's office on earth. The attending physicians will be all females, very gentle and extremely skilled. Using a special machine, they will beam a light right through your body; the light will search for your ovaries. You will feel nothing at all, it's just light, nothing will probe, or hurt, or even annoy you.

Once the light reaches the ovaries, it will activate one of the eggs, fertilize it, and have it move very smoothly into the uterus. You will then become pregnant, of course, and the fetus will begin to grow. Anunnaki women have the egg removed by the light, placed in a special tube, and grow the baby in a machine. They don't have birth in the same sense humans do, but take the baby home after he or she is ready in the advanced incubator.

However, in your case, since you are human, we thought it would be best not to tamper with your nature and allow you the full term, protecting the baby inside your body."

"Wow," I said. "That is not very scary at all... are you sure that is the way it goes? I heard such stories about alien abductions, and how they torment people with these probing machines."

"The other aliens, maybe. The grays, the reptilians, they are not too gentle and they don't particularly care how the humans feel. Still, many of the stories you hear might be a bit exaggerated. As for being sure about our procedures, why, yes, I have gone through that before, many times. I am perfectly sure. And my sister will be with you all the way."

"Did you ask any of the women to marry you?"

"No, I did not," said Marduchk.

"How come someone who looks like you never married?"

"I was married in another universe," said Marduchk, ignoring my remark about his looks in a gentlemanly manner.

"My other self is still married to his choice, of course, very happily so; they have three children, and I still watch them once in a while through the viewer. But I had to branch out, thirty thousand years ago, and now I am not married. Thirty thousand years is a very short time for an Anunnaki, you know. One needs time to make a decision about a life partner." I gave up.

I did not believe I will ever understand anything on Ashtari, and I was not going to question, at that moment, the issues of other selves and branching out to new universes... it made my head spin, so instead I ate another cookie. I was pleased he was not married in this universe, nonetheless.

After a short trip, lasting perhaps an hour, we landed on Ashtari. Before we went out, Marduchk said, "Don't be upset if you see nothing except swirling gray air. This is what happens to humans when they land here, and we can fix that in a couple of days. It is daylight now on Ashtari, the sun is shining. If necessary, just close your eyes." It all sounded a little ominous, but I found it was an understatement. The reality was much worse. I stepped out into a world which looked like a sand storm on a completely gray planet. It was horrible and it made me dizzy.

I swayed and grasped Marduchk's arm. "It's all right," he said reassuringly. "I will take you indoors right away."

We entered a building which I could not see, but inside, with a dim light, everything was clear and nice.

A lady came toward me, smiling, her hand extended to shake mine. She was gorgeous, tall, elegant, and looking remarkably like Marduchk, except that her hair was long and curly and glowed with a reddish sheen. She wore a beautiful long dress of deep sea green silk, and a long necklace of baroque pearls that glowed softly in myriad colors. "Welcome," said the lady.

"I am Sinhar Semiramicsh, Sinhar Marduchk's sister. Thank you for coming to Ashtari."

"Sinhar... Semi? I can't say it." I said weakly. Why are they both Sinhar, I was wondering. Later I found out that "Sinhar" is at the beginning of each name of an Anunnaki of high caste. It is similar to the habit of the Irish to precede names with "O'" and the Armenian habit of ending each name with "ian."

"Yes, I know," the lady smiled. "My human friends call me Miriam. Please do so, it will be easier."

169

"Yes, Miriam will be nice... But what is happening?" I asked, still dizzy. "Why can't I see anything outside?"

"It's the atmosphere. There is no pollution, no smoke, no oil fuels, since pure electromagnetic energy is all we use. It is so bright, so clear, that it creates a strange effect on your retina, which is used to different conditions. We are going to take care of it tomorrow morning. I would like you to rest, eat, and then sleep the night. Let me take her to her room, Sinhar Marduchk. The child is very tired from all this excitement."

"Of course," said Sinhar Marduchk. "Go with Miriam, Victoria, she will take good care of you, and I will see you in three days or so."

I looked around me.

The house was incredibly beautiful. The living room had very high ceiling, and there were platforms, or levels that ran smoothly into each other, each decorated with plants, little ponds, and flower basins. All the windows were covered with curtains, presumably for my sake, but it was clear that the windows were very large and normally admitted an enormous amount of light and air. I followed Miriam obediently to a smaller, very cozy room, which contained the most comfortable bed I have ever slept on and had sky blue ceiling and what seemed like hundreds of plants and flower vases.

She gave me a beautiful nightgown and robe to put on, and served me a light supper of a delicious fruit salad and something that tasted like yogurt.

I was tremendously excited, but to my amazement my eyes were literally closing with fatigue. Then, Miriam tucked me in bed like a mother, told me to have a good nap, and I slept instantly.

When I woke up, my treatment began. Miriam took me to a little room where she showed me a basin filled with aquamarine-tinted fluid. She asked me to go in, relax, and think only about colors, nothing else, preferably about one specific color. She would come back in an hour or so, she said, and the water will keep their gentle warmth as long as I was in.

I climbed into the bath which felt wonderful and was fragrant with some floral scent I did not recognize. I closed my eyes and thought about the color lavender, beautiful, gentle soft kind of lavender. For a while nothing happened, but after a few minutes, all of a sudden a stream of lavender light filled the basin and then lifted and surrounded me like a beautiful web.

To my surprise, at the same moment, a joint pain I developed on earth disappeared. It was in my ankle, which I have hurt a year ago while running, and it did not heel properly, giving me occasional pain. I twisted it when I left the spaceship and stumbled, and it hurt when I woke up from my nap. Now it was perfectly well. Later they explained that as they adjust the vision, they must cure all the weaknesses of the human body, my genes, and all the possible disease and sicknesses that I might have in the future. Even at my young age I could feel the difference between the human condition and perfect health.

On the second day, Miriam led me through a connecting corridor to a surgical room in another building. They have these corridors, connecting houses and buildings to each other, and they never lock any doors. Such a trusting, simple lifestyle, such a pleasure. She introduced me to a nurse, or physician, who asked me to lie down on a table.
I did, and a machine came from the ceiling, shining a laser-like beam. Apparently, they scanned my brain, and the nurse told me to look at the screen on my right side and see how the cells in my brain would create new visual faculties. This was utterly amazing. I could actually see how the human brain worked!
The nurse explained that many cells, millions of particles of the brains, are never used by humans, and now many of them would become mine to use. After a short time, the nurse put a bandage around my eyes and a metallic band around my forehead. This was needed for readjusting the energy and reactivating part of the cells. They told me that this will not only adjust my vision, but will develop a telepathic power in due time.
Indeed, to my great delight and astonishment, at a later day I was able to communicate telepathically with the Anunnaki, at will. When the treatment was completed, my vision was perfect, and Miriam told me that I could go out and see Ashtari for the first time.
Marduchk was waiting for us outside the door of the surgical room, and together the three of us went outside. I gasped. The air was pure, light, and full of rainbows of colors. I have never seen such colors, they were not known on earth. Some of the colors of the sky blended with the colors of the landscape, giving me the feeling that the ground united with the sky.

Then, I realized that something very strange was happening. My vision was not limited to straight lines. I could see, magically, to the left and right, like surrounding vision.

Gorgeous buildings glimmered under the brilliant sky, the trees, bushes, and flowers filled every available space, and beautifully dressed, smiling people walked in the streets.

How different from what I thought was a gray planet with swirling sand in its atmosphere! Later, I could very well understand when Marduchk told me that the colors blend with the psyche of the Anunnaki. They teach colors to children from a very early age, and it is so very important because understanding colors is essential for traveling through worlds and dimensions.

It was daytime, so the sun was shining. The whole celestial system is different on Ashtari, naturally. The day is not composed of twenty-four hours. It's made up of forty-eight hours. The sun rises around four o'clock in the morning, and the glorious sunrise takes about two hours; the colors at that time are beyond description.

The sun shines for eighteen hours, then takes two hours for sunsets that seem to burn the sky with their intensity. Then, they have four moons. All rise harmoniously one after the other, and line up in four different directions.

They stay for about ten hours. When they fade, it's again one after the other in the same synchronized manner, and the moonset is like molten silver filling the sky.

Then comes the night, but it is never one hundred percent dark. It's like deep dusk. The Anunnaki don't need full darkness because their eyes do not have the usual retina, but another structure. Even so, the stars are highly visible in the clear, clean atmosphere.

And now I was ready to enjoy myself.

Everyone I met was extremely friendly and charming, people treated me as if I was a hero of some sort, following a mission of great importance, and I liked being lionized. I did not have to worry about my parents, since I knew Marduchk will take me to earth one second after my car stopped, so I felt free, mature, and sophisticated, except that I was falling for Marduchk like a star-struck child. But I suppose that was to be expected by someone my age. Miriam gave me the most beautiful clothes to wear, and I would try them all before the mirror and be amazed at what they could do for my looks.

My nieces, Miriam's daughters, were of course much older than me but still children, according to Anunnaki life, so they were still very much interested in creating endless forms of things – flowers, plants, jewels, clothes – and we had the greatest fun. Only later, once they hit the age of seventy-one, Anunnaki become adults, and they lose their passion for creating endless forms and concentrate on the intellectual pursuits of their race, things like philosophy, poetry, and so on.

Not that they stop producing art, but it's done differently by the adults. They like frescoes, huge paintings. Nothing is miniature, all art is big, except jewelry, very well developed. For every color, they have four hundred different shades. And they have lots of huge sculptures.

Artists work on them in their studios, and students work on them in schools, and when they are done, they teleport it to public places for exhibitions. Physical labor is not part of the psyche of the Anunnaki. All is mental. They took me to the beautiful parks and gardens The Anunnaki are great gardeners, and constantly create new species of wonderful plants, both for food and for beauty. Children spend many years studying plants.

The children are extremely creative, appealing, and kind. They don't like or create weapons or not even sharp instruments. The idea of hurting or even annoying anyone does not even cross their minds, so they are capable of creating great beauty. The plants, by the way, don't follow the four seasons.

The trees and flowers bloom constantly and never die. Also, the color of the leaves changes according to the moods, feelings and thoughts of the person who planted it.

But there are no seeds, since the reproduction is so different on the Anunnaki world. Many of them look like the ones we have on earth, but their structure has major differences. No one waters them on Ashtari; there is no need.

They get nourishment and water directly from the air. Come to think of it, there is a similarity between the plants and the Anunnaki. Both find their energy in the air they breathe. The roses have no thorns.

The trees don't have bark, they are soft on the outside because many of them are used as a source of nourishment. Plants produce milk, oil, and Anbar, which is a delightful perfume.

To me it seemed that the nature of the world itself is friendly, working with the needs of the people who live on it.

I was thrilled with their houses, too. They are never high-rise, since the Anunnaki discovered that when the body is far away from the earth, it loses some of its energy. Nor do they like square rooms; everything is rounded, soft, flowing, and the houses have high ceilings.

Usually they contain several floors, but not in the usual boxed way, but divided into levels. They don't use stairs, the levels merge smoothly with each other. At every level, you see indoor pools and plants.

As I saw with the surgical room that Miriam took me to, one part of the house is always connected to the neighboring house though a corridor. This is done for the sense of unity, and they never have locks. The ceilings, by the way, change color with the seasons, to match the temperature outside. In winter, the ceiling is dark gray, and brings warmth. In summer, it becomes white, or the color of champagne. All is smooth and meant for comfort. For example, doors don't swing back and front, and never bang, rather they go up, sliding.

Materials used are natural stone, like marble or granite, and some trees that are grown especially for the purpose of building. One interesting stone is called ourjan, and its color is saffron.

Parts of it can be ground to make a good die to color clothes. To my amazement, they told me that on earth, the Phoenicians found it in the Mediterranean and called it ourjawan, also known as "the color of royalty," since on earth, absorbed by the murex shell in the Mediterranean and corrupted by salt, it is no longer saffron, but purple.

What I really found strange, more than anything else, was the issue of animals. The Anunnaki believe that the animals on earth were created by evil spirits, since animals are treated so badly by humans. The Anunnaki did not want to create animals. They were working in their genetic laboratories on creating new life forms for the human or quasi humans. Working often by trial and error, one formula produced cats.

They called them Bessa. Strangely, in Coptic, Arabic, and other Semitic language, the cat is called Bess.

Strange similarity for two separate civilizations that are apart by million light years! Somehow, only female cats were created, and the Anunnaki, who never hurt anyone or anything, let them live and actually started to like them very much.

They noticed that the cats responded to music and to the pleasant sound of falling water, something they always taught children to enjoy in school. But the cats, without training, appreciated what the educated and trained children do. And so the cats became great companions for the Anunnaki, and they live in most houses as part of the family.

One of the gifts that the Anunnaki gave the early friendly monarchs of the earth was a set of cats, trusting that these people will treat the cats well.

You can see that in the history and mythology of Egypt, where the cats were downright sacred, and that shows another connection between the lineage of the early pharaoh and the Anunnaki.

The cats of the Anunnaki have psychic powers, and although they don't sense fear and danger like earth cats, they predict weather. And another unique characteristic – they can talk. They talk to the Anunnaki in a language derived from the Anunnaki language.

It's simple, and uses only nouns, not adjectives or verbs. These conversations may be simple, but they are perfectly clear. The cats look a bit like our Siamese, but with pure white fur, and a rainbow of blue and gray around the neck. They are about double the size of earth cats, and the color of their eyes is very light blue.

The only other animals created by the Anunnaki, and that was done deliberately, are birds. Infinity of types and colors were created, and they all sing. Many of them give excellent eggs.

There are no insects, only butterflies, because they blend well with the beauty of the landscape and they were also created by genetic formulas. The genetic formulas are not carried on by advanced scientists, as on earth. The children create life forms.

It's part of their curriculum, but also it is a second nature for an Anunnaki to create. This extends to other materials – such as metal transmutation and solid matter vibes and frequencies.

According to their needs, they can change gold to iron, iron to silver, etc., depending entirely on necessity. On earth, we value diamonds and gold. On Ashtari, they are meaningless and without value, except for their prettiness and use as decorative materials.

The Anunnaki have other elements, minerals, and metals that are more important, because they are needed to create energy for spaceships, and for levitating and teleporting heavy weight blocks and materials.

Another thing I truly enjoyed were the libraries. Marduchk took me to one of them, a marvelous marble building, always opened for everyone to visit. The books, which seemed to be numbered in the millions, were not square like ours, but conical.

They were placed on shelves. You would go to the shelf, select your cone, and touch it with one finger. The cone would spin, throw out silvery light, and instantly you will absorb all its contents.

I could see spending eternity in such a place, who needed a university...but they had those as well, and I was going to visit them too, eventually. And the museums! So many museums.

Mostly, they displayed tools and apparatus that help the Anunnaki navigate different galaxies, past and present. Those I did not understand at all.

But I loved some other objects – they have instruments that produce musical sound never heard on earth. One note can be very high and very low at the same time, but the human ear cannot absorb it until some adjustments are made. Fortunately, my cure worked in this direction too, and I could enjoy the music. The high sound goes to right ear, and the low sound goes to the left ear. You have your own symphony. Many of these instruments do not even need playing, you just touch them and they give sounds. I spent hours experimenting with them.

But business was business, and although I was allowed to have fun, after about a week Miriam told me that everything was prepared for my fertilization.

I was to visit the hospital early in the morning, go through the procedure, rest the day, and then just have a good time on Ashtari until the birth.

I thought I was emotionally prepared, but the evening before the operation I was scared again. The fear struck me when Marduchk and I were strolling in one of the gardens, and suddenly I could not talk.

"Victoria, I can see you are not in the best of moods. Do you have second thoughts?

176

Tell me and I will immediately cancel everything and take you to earth. It's never too late to withdraw. This has to be entirely voluntary or not at all."

"I am scared, but it's not that I want to cancel. I am suddenly worried about having a baby, just like that, without being married... we don't do that easily. If my parents knew, they would be so horrified. On the other hand, if it were not for my parents, I would have maybe asked you to stay here with you and raise the baby, perhaps... I am so confused."

"First, the whole point is that the baby must be raised on earth, Victoria. By these particular parents. You were happy with your adoptive parents, right? Surely you trust that I would choose the perfect parents?"

"Yes, but..."

"And more important, you are not ready for such a decision, anyway. I would not want you to choose a certain life because you were dazzled by the new conditions, or because you imagine that you are emotionally involved. I would want you to choose such a life only when your feelings are real, concrete, finalized. Yes, I did ask you if you would feel better being married before you gave birth. But it was a mistake on my part, based on my compassion for your stress when we met."

"So you have changed your mind about marrying me?"

"I have not changed my mind. One never does. I will come back for you when you are thirty, and then I shall ask you to marry me. I have already made that choice. But my choice was not made lightly. Remember, I have known you for a very long time, since I watched over you for years, ever since they told me about your genetic makeup and your mission. In addition, I looked at what is available of your future self – the kind of woman you will become – though of course you don't understand as yet what I mean... So yes, I do know you very well, and I will ask you to marry me. But you cannot accept or reject me now – because your decision will not be based on true self knowledge."

"But that is mean, Marduchk. Thirty? That is twelve years from now! What if I get run over by a car and die at twenty-five?"

"Then I will make a skip in time, and come and get you five seconds before the car hits you," said Marduchk, laughing.

"Deal," I said, feeling better.

"And stop worrying about the operation. You will feel nothing."

I did not believe him and I stayed up all night, fretting. But he was right. The operation took thirty minutes, at most, the light found its way into my body with no trouble at all, did its thing, and I left the surgical table feeling as good as ever. Miriam came to get me, and we walked home for lunch, and that was that!

"So, now I have nine months vacation, right? What shall I do, other than romp with the children, dress up, and annoy you and Marduchk?" I asked as we were eating. "You will go to plays, to concerts, and to combination orchestra/dancing events, with musicians that are dancers, too, and carry on illustrative movements that extend the message of the music. I adore this form of entertainment and I think you will like it too.

You will get to know many charming people who will become dear friends and would welcome you if you decide to return to us. Marduchk will teach you as many ancient languages as you feel would help you in your studies on earth, and get you all the books you want to read. And we will all take the children to picnics and row on the canals, under the flowering trees."

"I love the canals. You have so much water on your planet."

"About fifty/fifty to the land, the ratio is, but we also have some wonderful water underground. I will show you the underground lakes, they are as blue as a sapphire, contained in glittering grottos. And how about swimming? Do you know that our oceans are sweet, not salty? Swimming is very nice."

"I will look like a whale, Miriam. I am pregnant, remember?"

"Not in the kind of bathing suit my daughter already designed for you. You will look like a mermaid."

"A very fat mermaid. Did you ever see a manatee, those sea cows, Miriam? Our sailors used to think they are mermaids. They are very fat..."

A visit with Sinhar Inannaschamra: I was now in my fourth month of pregnancy. I felt remarkably well, due to the incredible diet I was given.

I really should not call it a diet, it was more like a sophisticated, gourmet vegetarian cuisine, since on Ashtari they do not eat any meat, fish, or seafood.

They do have wonderful milk and cheese-like foodstuffs that are produced from a fruit that is much like a coconut, and excellent eggs from the variety of birds that flourish on Ashtari, but more

178

on that later, since I plan to devote an entire chapter to telling about the diet and lifestyle of the Anunnaki, which has so much to do with their longevity and perfect health, and it has done wonders for me.

These days, at age sixty, I look like a woman half my age, and I had not as yet needed to resort to any advanced Anunnaki technology to achieve that; after all, the Anunnaki can live up to 500,000 years, so I have no idea when I will need cell rejuvenation.
Come to think of it, while it is rare that the Anunnaki come to earth, sometimes, when they do, they may give the youth formula to someone and he or she can live to be over two hundred years old.
Human scientists have recently begun to say that earth people have the genetic capacity to live for a hundred and fifty years – truth is, they can live up to five hundred, if they choose the right formula...Incidentally, speaking of birds and cats, they are so unusual and have such astonishing traits that perhaps the flora and fauna of the planet Ashtari deserve their own chapter, too.
On that particular day, I went for an afternoon visit with Sinhar Marduchk's and Sinhar Semiramicsh's great grandmother. I call her great grandmother for lack of a better term, but she was quite a few generations further from being just the mother of their grandmother.
Sinhar Inannaschamra was immeasurably old, 400,000 years to be exact. Sinhar Inannaschamra sat under a shady tree, and she rose as she saw me and came to greet me.

A strikingly beautiful lady, she had masses of glossy black hair, piled up high on her head. Her skin was creamy and smooth, and her black eyes shown with wisdom and the joy of living.
She was tall and elegant and always beautifully dressed, this time wearing a crimson robe with a silver belt and heavy silver necklace and earrings, all bearing deep carving and symbols representing the secret powerful names of the Anunnaki first Creator – Aal-Khal Leck-Malkshrink-Nar.
I liked her very much from the moment we met, since she and I shared an interest.
She was an expert in human history, archaeology, mythology and folklore, subjects she taught at one of the great Ashtari academies.

_____

Her knowledge was acquired at first hand – she traveled over time and space, learning, observing, writing. Her books were masterpieces. I never stopped asking questions, and she delighted in imparting information, so we got along extremely well.

We settled ourselves under the beautiful tree that was looked very much like a willow, but in the curious way of Ashtari trees, was connected to two other trees of the same species; the trees there seem to nourish and feed each other.
Perhaps that is one of the reasons the trees constantly bloom and fruit. She served me some gorgeous fruit, Wer-Dah Nour-Mar. The name is quite poetic, it means "the flower or fruit of the light." She also handed me a delicate, almost transparent goblet made of onyx marble and filled with fragrant a rose water drink I found utterly delicious, named Ma-Ah Wer-Dah Anbar.

We ate and discussed our favorite subject. I already knew that the Anunnaki were not the first to experiment with and on humans, that about 145,000 years ago, the Igigihl, or Igigi, were the first extraterrestrials to create quasi-human specimens. But I wanted to know more about what I was told were grotesque experiments. "Yes," said Sinhar Inannaschamra. "At the very beginning of their genetic experiments, the results were catastrophic.
Their creations looked awful – bestial, very ugly, even frightening. This may have happened because the Igigi were more terrestrial explorers than geneticists, and therefore more interested in certain molecules found in terrestrial water, and in various minerals, than in creating a perfectly shaped human race."
"What were the Igigi like?" I asked. "Did they look like you?"
"Oh, no," said Sinhar Inannaschamra. "The Igigi did co-exist with the Anunnaki, and shared some traits with them, but they were totally dissimilar in their physical shape. They were huge, bigger even than the Anunnaki, but not graceful like them.
They had strong facial features and lots of hair. And believe me, their appearance was not enhanced by their outlandish clothes. Nothing elegant or pleasant, everything was made out of metal shields. They liked to adorn themselves with many iron bracelets and necklaces that sported some strange insignia that to anyone but an Igigi would be quite ominous... not a very attractive species. The Igigi were 245 million years older than the Anunnaki.

180

But you must hand it to them, they were highly advanced in mineralogy and minerals transmutation.

The Anunnaki were geneticists and engineers with a strong appreciation for aesthetics.

Therefore, the Igigi created a very primitive form of living beings on earth, exactly as you, the humans, created unappealing early forms and shapes of robots, and related mechanical devices, at the dawn of robotics. These robots were functional but not pretty to look at, and the Igigi considered the early quasi-humans to be not much more than machines with limited mental faculties."

"So what did the early humans look like?"

"Apes, really. You see, the earth was extremely cold at the time, and the Igigi had to cover the human bodies with lots of hair to protect them from the elements.

It took the quasi-human race thousands of years to evolve into an early human form, and even then not totally human, still looking like apes. Some of them had bizarre skulls and facial bones. I will show you pictures if you come to the Academy.

They actually experimented a bit with the early human-forms. First, they created the 'Nafar Jinmarkah' meaning 'individual on three legs.' They consisted of a very strong physical body but lacked agility. Those bodies were created to carry heavy weight.

The three legs' purpose was to support heavy loads they could lift and carry. Later on, the Igigi worked on a new human form that consisted of a body with two legs, to bring speed and better agility. Yet, early humans remained terrifying, nothing like the Biblical descriptions. The Igigi tried four times. I mean, they experimented in four different ways.

Each time, they faced a problem in designing the human skull. Early Igigi creators did not want to put brains in the skull so human-forms-bodies would not think... it was horrible.

Yes, you could consider these early human-forms as the world's first robots. The Anunnaki were the ones who created the brains for the humans. These early brains contained two million cells. But the Anunnaki too worked several times on the prototypes of humans.

In their final genetic experiments, the Anunnaki programmed humans with the thirteen original faculties."

"Did the Igigi treat the humans well?"

181

"Not really. They were pretty vicious toward the early quasi-human beings, treating them very badly."

"This is so different from what science and religion argue about on earth, Sinhar Inannaschamra," I said wistfully. "We don't seem to know much…"

"Well, the history and theories of human creation and evolution are distorted by both of you theologians and scientists," said Sinhar Inannaschamra. "But you can't blame them. Much of the evidence has been lost. Anyway, to understand the quasi-human race, one must know about the thirteen faculties."

"The quasi-humans' faculties?" I asked, a little confused.

"Yes. In the genes, molecules and DNA of the early quasi-human race, the Igigi programmed thirteen faculties, or functions.

The most important abilities were as follows:
- To move
- To sense danger
- To understand by association
- To memorize
- To see forms and shapes in four colors.

These colors were bright yellow, representing gold; grey, representing minerals and rocks; blue, representing the atmosphere, air, and water; and a very strong red, representing heat and blood. Other colors such as green, purple, lilac, etc, were not visible or known to the early and primitive form of quasi-humans."

"So they were not entirely primitive," I said.

"They were primitive enough…The first genetically created race could not speak, even the concept of language was wholly unknown to them.

Thousands of years later, the Anunnaki taught their own newly created race of humans to speak, read, and write. The Anunnaki's first genetically created human race was the seed of humanity as you know it; they began to populate the earth 25,000 years before the construction of the great pyramids.

I am only citing the pyramids as a landmark in human history to give you a chronological perspective. Greater, taller and bigger monuments were erected centuries before the construction of the pyramids, and some ruins can still be found in Phoenicia (Modern

Lebanon today) particularly in Baalbeck, and in Mesopotamia (Modern Iraq today). I have seen them all, at various stages of their development."

"How I would love to study like that. When I go back to earth, I will have to study the old fashioned way."

"It's a good start. Some day, when you come back to Ashtari, you will join the Academy and go on from there. Nothing is lost."

"Do you think I will ever learn to travel in time and see things in person?"

"Of course you will. We can easily teach you the skill, among others."

"How totally delightful that will be."

"You can visit endless points in time, learn the truth about so many things that are now obscure. And perhaps one day you will write a book about it, for your people, who knows?"

"I do so much hope so... I'd rather think about it than about my current mission."

"Do that, think happy thoughts. Your mission here is difficult, we all know that, but so important for the greater good. We honor you for accepting it."

I felt close to crying so I had to change the subject. "So tell me more about the real humans, please, Sinhar Inannaschamra," I said. "You know what we are taught. The scientists talk about evolution. The priests and rabbis talk about Adam and Eve. All of it so inaccurate."

"You are absolutely right," said Sinhar Inannaschamra. "As I mentioned before, they are not aware of so much of the truth of the matter.

Contrary to all beliefs, including what Judaism, Christianity and Islam teach you, Eve was not created from Adam's rib. Men were created from an early female form that was fertilized by the leaders and the elite of the Anunnaki in a very special way that we will discuss later. These women lived in quarantined cities, and had both sons and daughters thus fathered by the Anunnaki.

Some of the most puzzling sites of these cities, due to their size and functionality, were in Ur, Amrit, Ugarit, Petra (Batra), Tyre and Sidon. Early humans called the quarantined cities of these women 'The Cities of Mirage', and 'The Cities of Beautiful Illusion,' and the quasi-humans who were made out of earth were *not* allowed to interact with these women.

183

Thousands of years later, the inhabitants of what is today the Arab Peninsula and the lands bordering Persia, the United Arab Emirates, and India, called these women 'The Women of Light', and those who were allowed to mix with them were called 'The Sons of Light.'

From this early human race, all humans came to life. God had nothing to do with you. In other words, the God you know, revere, and fear today did not create you. Even the word or term 'God' did not exist in the early stages of the existence of the human race on earth.

Instead 'Gods' or 'Heavenly Masters' were used. And thousands of years later, those terms were changed to 'Giants,' 'Elohim,' 'Nephilim,' 'Anakim,' 'Fallen Angels,' you name it...Incidentally, the Early Anunnaki who visited earth were extremely tall. Some reached the height of 9 feet, and lived as long as 400,000 years. These Anunnaki did not leave descendants on earth. Those who came to earth much later, before the regional deluge, and right after that huge Tsunami, left families behind them when they returned home.

By home, I mean Zeta Reticuli and Ashartartun-ra. These families are the origin of the hybrids and/or extraterrestrial human beings living today among the people on earth. It is very important to learn and remember this.

Another important detail is the issue of population. For some reason, many believe that only grays or reptilians live on Zeta Reticuli, but this is not true at all. The Anunnaki had always occupied vast territories on Zeta Reticuli, and as you know they are not the grays or reptilians, as so wrongly described in Ufology literature."

"So many different races," I said.

"Indeed," said Sinhar Inannaschamra.

"Some 300,000 years before the creation of the cities of 'The Women of Lights,' forty-six different races of humans and quasi-humans populated the earth. The greatest numbers were found in Africa, Madagascar, Indonesia, Brazil, and Australia. These races died out not because of famine, ecological catastrophes, or acts of war, but because of the disintegration of the very molecules and composition of their cells. The Anunnaki created the 'final form' of human beings, and all of you are their descendents."

"I am rather surprised that records do not exist."

"Actually, they do, but they are well hidden.
There are those who know that the Sumerians, Ashurians, Hyskos, and Phoenicians are the direct descendants of the Anunnaki, and that their descendants carry a rather clean genetic pool, like you, my dear; you are practically a full Anunnaki, genetically. But they don't want it known, now as well as in antiquity.
For example, Eusebius, the Bishop of Cæsarea, Palestine, had genealogical records of the descendants of the Anunnaki who became Syriac.
At the Council of Antioch in 363 CE, Bishop Eusebius intended to bring this subject in his *Theophania* to the attention of the members of the Council. But no additional information or manuscripts about what happened at the Council were provided.
In the Syriac manuscripts of Zachariah of Mitylene, who frequently corresponded with Eupraxius, two references were made to the Anunnaki as the ancestors of the Ashurian-Syriac. Another bishop by the name of Proterius tried to destroy these letters.
Fortunately, two hand-written copies were made, as the tradition of this era dictated, and were saved in the vault of a scribe. Those letters resurfaced in 1957 in a personal acquisition of Cardinal Maouchi, the Patriarch of the Maronite Church in Lebanon.

After Maouchi's death, those files were kept in the secret vaults of Al-Kaslik Monastery in Lebanon. As for modern knowledge, the original language of the Anunnaki is still intact and is currently used by top American scientists and researchers who work in secret American-Alien military bases in the United States and Mexico.
In 1947, the first attempt was made by American linguists, who previously worked at the OSS (Precursor to the CIA), to decipher it.
They tried to compare it with the Sumerian, Hebrew, Armenian and Phoenician Alphabet, languages which are directly derived from the Anunnaki's written language. The problem they faced and could not resolve were the geometrical symbols included in the written Anunnaki's texts.
But in 1956, they cracked the code.
Those mathematical figures hold great secrets regarding an alien advanced technology used for peaceful and constructive purposes.

The American military intelligence and what's left from Dr. Fermi's group at Los Alamos wanted to use this alien technology for military purposes."

"The language is in use? Now?"

"Oh, yes. The American top military scientists who work in secret military bases and aliens' laboratories on earth have an extraterrestrial lexicon, and use it constantly. In that lexicon, or dictionary, you will find variations of Phoenician and Sumerian symbols. Some letters represent maritime and celestial symbols and measurements. The fact that the Americans are still using this extraterrestrial language should be enough to convince anyone that extraterrestrials, Anunnaki and Zeta Reticuli descendants, still live among you, otherwise why would anyone learn a language that cannot used to communicate with people who speak it and write it?"[1]

"Who else has a strong connection to the Anunnaki?" I asked.

"Besides the Sumerians, the Phoenicians, the Hyksos, and the Philistines, there are indeed others, such as the very early Etruscans, Druids, Minoans, and people of Mu.

Later, the Ashurians resided among the last remnants of the Anunnaki who visited earth and lived there for 600 more years. After that, the Anunnaki left earth for good, to return only as visitors. One of the reasons for their departure was the discovery of the 'tree of life,' also known as 'The Tree of Knowledge' by humans – a metaphor for the acquisition of knowledge and understanding by the human race, on its own. The acquisition of this supreme knowledge caused the humans to rebel against the Anunnaki."

"What a mistake," I said. "Had we stayed loyal to the Anunnaki, we could have spared ourselves so much grief."

"Yes, but that is the way humans are, I am afraid... but as I said, we love you anyway."

---

[1] On some of the manifestos of military parts used in anti-gravity secret laboratories underground in the United States, several letters were borrowed from the 'Enuma Elish' of Sumeria and regularly appeared on the top right corner of each document. In the eighties, those Sumerian numbers were replaced by an Americanized version.

"I understand that there is a close relationship between your language and your religion, is it not so?"
"Yes, it is. The Anunnaki have two kinds or styles of languages; one is spoken and the other one is written. The spoken language is the easiest one to learn, and it is used by the Anunnaki's population.
The written one is used in books exclusively and consists of twenty-six letters. Seven of these letters represent the planets that surround our star.

Many of the Anunnaki's letters cannot be pronounced by humans, because of certain limitations of your vocal chords. There are seven additional letters that are complete words, and these words represent the attributes of our 'Grand Leader.' Translated into terrestrial language, the Grand Leader is the creator of energy, in other words, 'God.'
However, the Anunnaki do not believe in a God in the same sense you do, even though they were the ones who created and originated the early forms of religions on earth.
However, those Anunnaki that have brought religion to earth were of a lower class.
The god they brought was a vengeful and terrifying god, something that the Gnostics and early scholars of the Coptic Church in Egypt were fully aware of. The doctrines show their disdain for such a god, and consequently, they called him the 'Creator of Evil and Darkness.'

Later on in history, the Gnostics began to spread the word that this earth was not created by the God of the Church, but rather by an evil demi-god. The early human beings who interacted with the Anunnaki shared similar beliefs."
"If humans learn about all this, the religious aspect would be most difficult to reconcile," I said.
"And yet, there is so much that is in common," said Sinhar Inannaschamra. "For example, your human ancestors borrowed many words from extraterrestrial languages, and learned the secret seven powerful names of God.
Many of the Phoenician linguists and early creators of their Alphabet borrowed numerous words and expressions from the higher class of the Anunnaki.

187

Ancient Phoenician texts and poems, recorded on tablets found in Tyre and Sidon, included reference to symbols and words taken from the written language of the upper class of the Anunnaki. Members of an early Anunnaki expedition to Phoenicia taught the Phoenicians how to develop their language, and revealed to them the secret powerful names and attributes of Baalshalimroot.
They instructed them not to use these words for ill purposes.
Particularly, the word 'Baalazamhour-Il' is never to be said, spelled, or written.
Later on in history, the Hebrews religiously observed this instruction, and pronouncing the word of name of God became forbidden. However, the Anunnaki revealed to the Phoenicians and Sumerians seven positive and powerful names/attributes of the Grand Leader. If well used, these words can bring prosperity, good health, and salvation in moments of difficulty. The prophet Mohammad learned these seven words from an early Christian ascetic, a Sahara hermit called Raheb Bouhayra.

Today, Muslims all over the world are aware of these seven words or names. They call them in written Arabic 'Asma' Al Lah Al Sabha' Al Housna,' meaning the seven lovely names of God. Those names do not have numerical value or secret meanings as many scholars claim, simply because they were not originally written in a geometrical form.
None of these words appeared in the so-called hieroglyphic measuring tape that the Americans found at the crash site in Roswell. The symbols and geometrical signs Americans found in Roswell were biochemical symbols.
Also, early names of the Hebrew God were of an extraterrestrial origin.
It is true that the Sumerian ancient texts and records mentioned names of some of the Anunnaki leaders such as Utu, Ningishzida, Ninki, Marduk, Enki, Enlil, Inanna, but the greatest name of all remains Baalshalimroot, also referred to as 'Baalshalimroot-An'kgh.' Terah, the father of Abraham, mistakenly worshiped Baalshalimroot-An'kgh. Early Semites made the same mistake when they worshiped the leaders of the Anunnaki as gods who later became Bene Ha-Elohim, meaning the children of the gods. The Anunnaki never introduced themselves as gods.

The words: El Elyon and Yahweh or Jehovah were taken directly from the Anunnaki's written language. The original word was "Yah'weh-El' Ankh" and El Elyon was "Il Ilayon-imroot."
"It's hard to understand the difference between lower class and upper class Anunnaki, not to mention the other races," I said. "It is, actually, quite bewildering."

"I know, it's rather difficult... some of your scholars equated the Anunnaki with the Nephilim. This is not totally correct. The lower class of the Anunnaki are the Nephilim, although many historians call them sometimes Anakim or Elohim.
The higher class of the Anunnaki is ruled by Baalshalimroot, and his followers or subjects are called the 'Shtaroout-Hxall Ain,' meaning the inhabitants of the house of knowledge, or 'those who see clearly.'
The word 'Ain' was later adopted by the early inhabitants of the Arab Peninsula. 'Ain' in Arabic means 'eye'.

In the secret teachings of Sufism on earth, visions of Al Hallaj, and of the greatest poetess of Sufism, Rabiha' Al Adawi Yah, known as 'Ha Chi katou Al Houbb Al Ilahi' (The mistress of the divine love), and in the banned book *Shams Al Maa'Ref Al Kubrah* (Book of the Sun of the Great Knowledge), the word 'eye' meant the ultimate knowledge, or wisdom from above.
'Above' clearly indicates the heavens. Later on, it was used to symbolize the justice of God or 'God watching over us.' And much later in history, several societies and cultures adopted the 'eye' as an institutional symbol and caused it to appear on many temples' pillars, bank notes, money bills, and religious texts. "I think even now these symbols are still around, Sinhar Inannaschamra," I said.
"It is fascinating how such things stick around."
"Absolutely. Your Freemasons' and Illuminati's favorite symbol is the Anunnaki's eye. And as everything changes in time and takes on different forms and meanings, the 'eye' became a 'triangle,' a very secretive and powerful symbol.
George Washington carried this triangle with him wherever he went, and wore it during official ceremonies. If you double and reverse the triangle, you get the Star of David.

189

This very triangle is visible on many extraterrestrial spacecrafts, and on uniforms of military personnel in secret American military bases underground, working on alien technology and propulsion systems. And it will stay on, I am sure. As an example, on February 17, 1953, an American millionaire by
the name of Paul Warburg who was involved with the triangle issues shouted before the Senate of the United States of America: 'We shall have world government whether or not you like it, by conquest or consent.'"

"Sounds rather ominous," I said. "Yes, the 'Triangle' can be a negative force," said Sinhar Inannaschamra.

"When integrated without balance and cosmic harmony, in other words, spatial equilibrium, in architectural design and lining up territories, the triangle becomes a negative force on the map. If the three sides of the triangle are separated, such separation can cause serious health problems.

The triangle becomes three lines of negative energy. This energy is not easily detected; nevertheless it runs strong and deep underground.

People who live above these lines suffer enormously. In many instances, this negative power or current can negatively affect the present and future of many human beings.

Similar to some Ufologists who can identify UFOs' hot spots on earth, usually above ground, descendants of the extraterrestrials can identify and locate the negative currents underground. Each country has these negative currents or circuits underground. I do not wish to scare you, my dear, but I must inform you that some American states are located above these lines.

For example, Mississippi, Alabama, the northern part of Washington, DC, and two areas in Brooklyn, New York share this misfortune."

"Scary," I said. "Poor people, suffering for no fault of their own."

"Many manage to overcome by sheer strength of character and goodness," said Sinhar Inannaschamra. "Life is full of challenges for everyone."

"Life here seems very pleasant," I said.

"Yes, in many ways it is," said Sinhar Inannaschamra. "And yet, we all have our burdens. But let's think of nicer things. How about a stroll in the garden?

I would like to show you a nest of the most gorgeous new little birds; their parents trust me, I always feed them good things, so they will not object.

We must take some of these almonds for them..." and so we went for a stroll in the magnificent garden, and the lesson was over for the day as soon as a tiny bird, all gold and red, flew clumsily out of the nest and perched on my finger.

"She must be the first to take wings," said Sinhar Inannaschamra proudly, as the parent birds sat on her hands and delicately nibbled at the delicious almonds.

The sky was turning purple as the three moons of Zeta Reticuli started to set, the soft light giving way to darkness, and the scent of the night blooming flowers began to permeate the air.

An irrevocable decision: How I had to choose between giving up my child for the common good of humanity or be transported to another universe, away from everyone I loved.

And that, I thought, was that. The next day was my scheduled birth time. I was ready, and I was confident that I would not suffer under the gentle care of the Anunnaki physicians. I knew them all well now, they became my good friends, and whenever I needed to be examined, or have a little treatment, I was not even afraid and rather enjoyed visiting these ladies. I would feel nothing, that is, nothing physical.

Emotionally, that was another question altogether.

The thought of giving up my baby was preying on me. Perhaps the psychological burden was even greater because I was an adopted baby myself, I really can't tell, but I was more and more uneasy about it. And yet, it was a point of honor to say nothing about my feelings.

I did not want to distress either Miriam or Marduchk, who had invested so much time, effort, and work in the project. And so at dinner I made a special effort to be cheerful and pleasant, and I really thought I managed to cover my feeling and dupe Miriam and her daughters into thinking that all was well. Marduchk was not there; it somehow made me unhappy, I wanted to see him that evening before the great event, but according to Miriam he had to attend some function of great importance in the great library they called the Akashic Library, where all the knowledge of the universe was supposed to be accumulating for eons.

191

I was promised that some day in the far future I could see it, and I was curious about it, but right now it was the furthest thing from my mind and I was sad not seeing Marduchk.

I snuck out for a quiet walk in the garden while the Miriam and her daughters were admiring a new picture the girls created, telling them I wanted to do my meditation exercises.

I sat on one of the white marble benches, covered with gorgeous crimson and gold pillows, and really prepared to do my meditation exercises that the physicians taught me as a way to relax body and soul. I wish I could say I stuck with it, but instead, I started crying uncontrollably. After a short while, I felt a hand on my shoulder. Startled, I turned around and saw Marduchk.

"Marduchk! I am so glad to see you! I thought you will be busy all evening at the Akashic Library!" I sniffed and snuffled and tried to stop crying.

"I got away as early as I could. I wanted to see you before the big day tomorrow, and Sinhar Semiramicsh told me you were in the garden. But you are greatly distressed, Victoria. Let's talk about it, and see if I can help."

"I don't know, Marduchk," I said, wiping my eyes. "I don't even know how to explain... it's all so difficult..."

"Well, let's try to make it easier. There are always many options."

"Do you mean I can change my mind, even now?" I asked. "But the baby is due tomorrow!"

"Yes, you can change your mind," said Marduchk. "I will not lie to you and say that it will be easy, but it is doable."

"How?" I said.

"I can take you, still pregnant, to another dimension, another universe, and you will keep the baby."

"But what about my parents? They will not know what happened to me."

"They will have your former self. That one would have never met me, and life would go on as usual for the three of them." That was extremely confusing, but I thought I understood. Marduchk will travel back in time, and change the past.

The girl that was I, the one that drove the car, would just go on driving, never meet Marduchk, while I, the offshoot, will be here, on Ashtari.

Maybe.

I could not concentrate on that, because the really important question was very different, and I needed to know that right away.

"Will I ever see you again, Marduchk?"

"No, you will not. That would be impossible, each of us will be living in different dimension." That thought really hurt, and his tone of voice and the look on his face told me it was irrevocable.

"So what would happen to me in the new universe?"

"I will find you a husband. You would believe that you married for love and that this man was the father of your baby, and you will live a normal human life there."

"And you will stay here."

"Yes, I will have to stay here, give you up, both from the point of view of the project, and worse, personally. That will be the price. That is why I said it would not be easy."

"You could not come with me to the new universe?"

"No. I cannot do so. I have only been here for thirty thousand years, Victoria, since my last branching.

A blink of an eye in Anunnaki life. I have obligations, which cannot be left undone without enormous damage to many people, both Anunnaki and Human."

"Don't you care about losing me, Marduchk?"

For a long while he was silent, just sitting there, staring at ground. Then he said, "Yes, I would care very much. It will be more difficult for me than you can even begin to imagine. But an Anunnaki does not break his word, and does not walk out on his obligations."

"But humans do, right?"

"Sometimes," he said.

"And if I decide not to give up the baby, if I decide to move on to that new universe, I will be breaking my word to the Anunnaki."

"We will not hold it against you, Victoria. Never."

I took a deep breath and made my final decision. It was very hard, but it had to be done. I looked up at him and said, "I will not break my word either, Marduchk. The birth will go on as planned tomorrow, no matter how I feel. I have my obligations too."

The relief in Marduchk's black eyes was almost palpable. He could barely speak, it seemed.

Finally he said simply, "Thank you, Victoria," and then put his head in his hands and was silent for a while.

"I am very, very grateful," he added. "And since you made the decision yourself, after receiving honest information, I feel your free will was exercised without any coercion."

"I did exercise my free will, Marduchk." There was no coercion, but I have to admit, so many years later, that the thought of losing Marduchk was at least as strong in my decision as the idea of honoring my obligations. I am not as noble as Marduchk, probably never will be.

"I want to make your situation a bit easier for you, though. There is no need for you to suffer emotionally. Let me make you forget everything from this evening on.

I will wipe your memory, take you to your room, and tomorrow everything will be done as planned. The next thing you will see will be the old Maine road as you drive home."

"So we will say goodbye tonight, Marduchk?"

"If you agree to this plan."

"I like the plan. It's quite merciful. But would you do me a favor, first?"

"Of course."

"Please try to explain to me, in the simplest fashion, this issue of branching and changing universes. Particularly, I want to understand the marriage you told me about."

"The marriage? Why?"

"Well, you see, in the future your personal life may be quite important to me, even the previous one. I will need to know such things, or they may burden my mind with questions and doubts.

Now, I realize that if you explain everything now, I will promptly forget it, but as soon as my memory is returned, it will be there quite safely. And then we won't have to discuss the past, just move on into the future."

"That makes sense," said Marduchk. "As a matter of fact, this is a very mature and intelligent consideration.

You are human, and the issue of trust is sensitive with humans, since their relationships are not as permanent as ours.

Do you know, Victoria, we don't even have words for infidelity, or mistress, or extramarital affairs, or cheating? Once we make our choice, it is so permanent, it is as simple and as obvious as the air we breathe. But of course you need a different kind of reassurance. It's only natural, but it will all change. In a few hundred years, such thoughts will disappear from your mind altogether."

194

"So what happened to you?"

"Well, first you must understand the concept.

The closest metaphor in human terms would be that sometimes, you wish you could do something differently, change the past, change a life decision, right?"

"Yes, like, perhaps, going back in time to a point before you made a bad decision."

"Exactly. Or, if you think that you could do some good if you changed an entire event.

Well, in our case, we do have the solutions for these dilemmas. We can split ourselves in two, or more if necessary, and move on to a universe that is very much like the one we are leaving."

"One universe which is like the one you are living in... does that mean there are so many universes, that some of them do not resemble this one?"

"Yes. There is an infinite number of universes. If you wish to branch and move, you have to study the matter very carefully and make the right selection."

"And the branching, or splitting, results in exact copies of the same person?"

"Yes, at the moment of separation.

After that, each grows, spiritually, in a different direction, follows his or her own free will and decisions, and eventually the two are not exactly alike."

"So what do they do, first of all?"

"The old one stays where he is and follows his old patterns as he wishes. The new one might land one minute, or a month, or a year, before the decision he or she want to change or avoid."

"So let me see. Thirty thousand years ago, you decided that something was wrong in your life?"

"Not wrong, exactly. I was living a nice life with my wife and family. But I felt that I did not accomplish much, that I chose an easy life of playing with poetry and literature, and I suddenly wanted to be more active in the development of the universe."

"What do you think caused this change?"

"I witnessed a horrendous event, Victoria.

A certain group of beings in our galaxy destroyed an entire civilization wantonly, killing millions of the inhabitants, in order to take over their planet for mining purposes.

It happened while I was on a trip, and I actually saw the explosions while I was traveling.
It was quite traumatic, and I thought, at that moment, that I must be active in preventing such events from occurring again, ever."
"So you told your wife, and what did she say?"
"My wife did not want to change our lifestyle, she was very happy just as she was, and if I changed my own life it would have caused her much pain.
I would never want that to happen. But the restlessness was constant, and so my wife and I consulted, and together we decided that branching would be the perfect solution. I would go back in time to be in a spot before that fateful trip, branch out, and leave my former self, who was happy and content, to get on with his pleasant life. I, on the other hand, that is, the new person, would come to this universe, and start fresh, doing what I want to do."
"And you have accomplished what you wanted?"
"I have only just begun, but yes, I work hard."
"And for thirty thousand years, no one was right for you to marry, in this universe."
"Thirty thousand years are not a very long time to find the perfect life partner."
"Well, so now I understand," I said. "And do you hear from your wife and family?"
"At first, just to make sure all was well, I viewed them occasionally on one our viewing machines. Not any more, though. I don't want to spy on their privacy. They seemed as happy as ever, and that is all that matters."
"I think I do understand now, Marduchk," I said. "Not the technical parts, of course, that is beyond me. The idea of splitting a person, branching, is rather alien to me."
"I think you understand the principle, though," said Marduchk.
"You know, Marduchk, for someone who is 300,000 old, and so intellectually superior to me, it is amazing, and really pleasant, how much you treat me as an equal. At my age, you could have treated me as if I am a fly on the wall."
"But you are my chosen life partner, Victoria. Naturally I would treat you with all the respect you deserve. Besides, as you know, I have glimpsed into the future and I know the kind of woman you will be in a few hundred years, if you decide to come back to me."

"And yet, I am not allowed to accept or reject the marriage proposal."

"It won't be fair to you. You will not be exercising complete free will."

"Very well. But could you give me a small example of what it would be like to be married to you? I mean, show me what the merging of lights will be like? Now don't give me that alarmed look, as if I am breaking a horrible taboo.

I don't mean the whole thing, of course, that is not allowed unless we are married, but just a little sample."

"But won't it influence your free will too?"

"I can't see why it should. It would not do more than a date, kissing me good night, could influence my choice of a husband years later."

"Even a small sample would be more than that," said Marduchk.

"Let's just take a chance for once," I said.

"It might influence your ability to choose and love a human man," said Marduchk.

"I certainly hope so," I said. "Do you realize what I will be missing if I meet and marry a human man?"

"But what about free will?"

"Free will may be overrated in this case, Marduchk. Besides, you will make me forget, deeply forget, one hundred percent forget. You know you can do it."

"I can't refuse it," said Marduchk. "I hope I am doing the right thing. But right or wrong, I simply can't refuse. So, just give me your hands, but sit as far away from me as you can. We don't want the light to catch on to the rest of our bodies, just the hands. And that, Victoria, must be our goodbye – for a while."

"You will make me forget after the lights merge?"

"Yes. Then, I will take you to your room, tell Miriam that you are not conscious to your surroundings, and tomorrow we will take care of business. I will be back for you, Victoria. Trust me on that."

I nodded and extended my hands, and he took them between his own. I felt a slight warmth, but for a while it seemed to be just the normal physical contact of hands.

Then, I saw a glowing golden light rising from our joined hands. I am not sure if any words exist that could do justice to how this felt, try as I might.

There was a sensation of magnificent physical well-being, mingled and combined with a sudden understanding that everything would be all right, that the universe is working as it should and that I could allow myself to be a part of it, totally and fearlessly.

The pleasure that this combination of physical and spiritual joys produced was extremely intense, and I clearly remember thinking that if that was just a small sample of what marriage to an Anunnaki can be, well, the real thing was well worth waiting for...

I felt as if my entire being was blazing, and then everything vanished, swept into a soft, velvety dark night that smoothly turned into an evening on a lonely stretch of road in Maine, and I was blissfully driving home from an afternoon study with my best friend.

But something remained. I am certain of it, and no matter how many times Marduchk later swore to me that my memory was completely stopped, still something remained, some remnant of this incredible feeling that would guide and keep me in the twelve years that were to follow until we met again.

And if you ask me, that beats free will every time.

*** *** ***

Published by

Times Square Press
New York, Berlin
Website: www.timessquarepress.com

Printed in the
United States of America and Germany
2014

.

www.ingramcontent.com/pod-product-compliance
Lightning Source LLC
Chambersburg PA
CBHW022359280326
41935CB00007B/238